Collins

WATERV

Norfolk Broads

Published by Nicholson
An imprint of HarperCollins*Publishers*
Westerhill Road, Bishopbriggs,
Glasgow G64 2QT

email: nicholson@harpercollins.co.uk
www.harpercollins.co.uk
www.bartholomewmaps.com

Copyright © HarperCollins*Publishers* Ltd 2010

Wildlife text from *Collins Complete Guide to British Wildlife* and *Collins Wild Guide*.

This product uses map data licensed from Ordnance Survey® with the permission of the Controller of Her Majesty's Stationery Office. © Crown copyright 1999. All rights reserved. Licence number 399302.

Ordnance Survey is a registered trade mark of Ordnance Survey, the national mapping agency of Great Britain.

The representation in this publication of a road, track or path is no evidence of the existence of a right of way.

Researched and edited by Cicely Frew.

The Publisher gratefully acknowledges the assistance given by the Broads Authority in the preparation of this guide, in particular Hilary Franzen and Tom Barrett.

Printed in China by South China Printing Co. Ltd.

ISBN 978-0-00-735831-1

Imp 001

INTRODUCTION

The Broads (the Norfolk and Suffolk Broads) are one of Britain's best-known holiday boating areas. They make up Britain's largest and most important protected wetland and are a national park providing a home to some of the rarest plants and animals in the country. A unique and enchanting wetland, with over 200 km (125 miles) of lock-free, navigable tidal waters, all waiting to be explored.

The area extends over the lower reaches of the Rivers Waveney, Yare and Bure, together with the Rivers Ant and Thurne (tributaries of the Bure) and the River Chet (the tributary of the Yare). The low-lying, wetland landscape contains around 60 shallow lakes. These lakes are referred to as 'broads', while we use the term 'the Broads' to refer to the entire area.

The history of the familiar landscape we see today dates back to the Middle Ages in the form of written evidence of peat digging in the Broads. By this time, much of the area had been cleared of woodland for fuel and building material. In the 12th century peat digging had become a major industry, the cut turfs being used for fuel. Almost every Broads settlement had its own pit, from where the peat was extracted on a huge scale. Gradually sea levels rose and the pits flooded making cutting more difficult until, by the 14th century, the peat diggings were abandoned.

For a long time, the origins of the broads were not properly understood. In 1952 Dr J M Lambert advanced the theory that these waterways were, in fact, man-made: a suggestion received with scepticism. However, researchers discovered that the sides of the broads were vertical, not gently sloping as would be the case with a naturally formed lake: evidence that these immense areas of water had originally been dug by hand. This was supported by the knowledge that there had been a massive demand for peat in the area, which by the 14th-century was both densely populated and prosperous.

Historically, the Broads' economy was centred on agriculture and the profitable wool trade. The marshman's way of life exploited the natural landscape of the lowland river valleys by tending cattle, cutting reeds, building dykes and drainage mills, harvesting fish and hunting wildfowl.

In the 16th-century, Norwich, after London, was the second largest city in England, its wealth built on wool, weaving, fishing, agriculture and general trade. There was a large export market from Norwich via Great Yarmouth and the waterways – natural and man-made – were major trading routes essential for communication and commerce, not only for meeting the large market for goods outside of the area but for local communication supplying the riverside settlements.

The distinctive Norfolk wherries (*see* page 5 for a brief description) were developed to navigate this area of rivers and lakes, and for several hundred years provided essential transport. The coming of the railways in the 1870s started the decline in commercial sailing, as the area's transport system was developed and cargo-carrying was transferred to the trains. However, the railways also opened up the Broads to recreation and enterprising wherry owners converted their vessels to accommodate passengers in order to make up lost income. Inhabitants of the Broads had always used the waterways for pleasure, alongside their day-to-day work and these early wherry conversions were the start of the tourism business that has continued to expand over the years and now sees around two million visitors enjoying the Broads annually.

However, the ensuing decades of increasing visitor numbers, boating and intensive agriculture had a detrimental effect on the fragile environment of this area. By the 1950s the clear Broads water had become cloudy and polluted, the river banks were eroding and the unmanaged fenland was turning into scrub. After alarming reports on the degradation of the Broads, the original Broads Authority was created in 1978 to manage the area.

Following considerable success in dealing with the environmental problems and tackling restoration, this organisation was granted Special Statutory Status in 1988 and in 1989 the Broads were given equivalent status to a National Park, one of 15 specially protected areas within the UK. The Broads Authority has three main aims: to conserve and enhance the natural beauty, wildlife and cultural heritage of the Broads; to promote opportunities for the understanding and enjoyment of the special qualities of the Broads by the public; to protect the interests of navigation. The Authority also has responsibility for the needs of agriculture and forestry and the economic and social interests of those who live or work in the Broads.

This guide is designed to help visitors plan their visit to the Broads in advance and to be a practical reference while exploring the area. For many people, the best way to discover the Broads is by boat and this book describes the varied ways in which you can get onto the water in all types of craft, whether for an hour's boat trip, for a week-long boating holiday, a day's canoeing or simply by hiring a rowing boat. Of course, not everyone wants to take to the water so we have also included lots of information for the casual visitor as well as those wishing to explore the area on foot or by bicycle, or to enjoy a day's fishing. There are also chapters listing places to eat and places to visit. The unique wildlife of the Broads is included too, with a chapter describing some of the plants and creatures that may be seen on land and in the water.

Please note that distances given are approximate and that conversions are rounded up to the nearest 0.5 km or mile.

Ted Ellis, one of Norfolk's best-loved naturalists and broadcasters, described the Broads as 'a breathing space for the cure of souls'. We hope that this guidebook will encourage you to explore the Broads, enjoy their unique atmosphere and special qualities, and to find your own breathing space.

If you would like to comment on any aspect of the guide, please write to Nicholson Waterways Guides, Collins Geo, Westerhill Road, Bishopbriggs, Glasgow G64 2QT or email nicholson@harpercollins.co.uk.

Halvergate Marshes (page 54)

Whether you are an experienced sailor or are completely new to boating, the Broads will provide you with the perfect way of getting onto the water. Boats of all types, large and small, can be hired by the hour or day, for short breaks and for whole weeks.

The Broads Authority publishes *Code of Conduct* leaflets for canoeing, rowing, sailing and day boat cruising. The leaflets offer simple tips and information to help make your trip a safe and enjoyable experience.

BOAT HIRE

Please book a boating holiday from a licensed operator – only in this way can you be sure that you have proper insurance cover, service and support during your holiday. It is illegal for private boat owners to hire out their craft. The Broads Authority website and their Information Centres provide information on hire companies. Take a look at the Where to Hire chapter of this guide (*see* page 70), for a full list of what is available for hire, together with operators providing tuition. Extensive information and advice on booking a boating holiday is available from the Inland Waterways Association (*www.waterways.org.uk*).

Full instruction is always provided when you hire any craft. Take notes, follow the boatyard's instructions and don't be afraid to ask if there is anything you do not understand. You could also consider signing up for a training course, *see* Where to Get More Information, page 24.

ELECTRIC BOATS

Electric boats are quiet and better for the environment than ordinary motor boats. They are available for hire and the Broads Authority also offers boat trips onboard electric boats.

CANOES

Paddling your own canoe is a unique way to get up close to nature. Canadian canoes can be hired from centres across the Broads. No previous experience is necessary and the canoes are suitable for families with children. Life-jackets are included in the hire price. Pre-planned itineraries and routes are available. The British Canoe Union (*www.bcu.org.uk*) can provide details of training courses for beginners.

MOTOR BOATS

Motor boats to suit everyone from couples to large families can be hired from the many hire centres and boatyards around the Broads. All the necessary safety equipment is included in the price of hire, together with on-board facilities ranging from the basic to the luxurious.

SAILING YACHTS AND DINGHIES

Don't let a lack of experience put you off having a go at sailing. If you have a little experience – even in the smallest dinghy – you will quickly learn to handle a sailing cruiser, and, as with all types of boat hire, full instruction will be provided. Several boatyards around the Broads offer trips with qualified skippers.

Canoeing at Salhouse (page 43).

On the water near Beccles (page 65).

WINDSURFING

The best places to launch are at Oulton Broad (page 66) and the purpose-built beach at Hickling Broad (page 40) where a small fee is charged. Courses are available at Whitlingham Outdoor Education Centre (page 50).

SAILING SCHOOLS

Even if you have no sailing experience at all, various centres offer expert tuition in sailing, canoeing and windsurfing. The generally quiet waters of the Broads are an ideal area in which to learn to handle a sailing boat and you can concentrate on the art of sailing without worrying about navigation. The chapter Where to Hire (*see* page 70) lists organisations and boat yards offering tuition within the Broads area. The Royal Yachting Association offers accredited courses all over the country. These include tuition in small and large boat sailing, motor cruising and windsurfing. Visit their website (*www.rya.org.uk*) for more details.

BOAT TRIPS

If you are not hiring your own boat, many places offer boat trips and guided tours of the Broads. The Broads Authority operates several electric boat trips, allowing you to explore some of the most beautiful nature reserves in the area. It is advisable to book these trips in advance. For a full list of boat trips, *see* Where to Hire, page 70.

Electric Eel **Wildlife Water Trail** (page 44) *Near Ludham, Great Yarmouth, Norfolk NR29 5PG (01692 678763 to book; www.broads-authority.gov.uk).* Explore How Hill Nature Reserve on an Edwardian-style electric boat. *See also* Places to Visit, page 92.

Helen of Ranworth (page 43) *Ranworth Staithe, Ranworth, Norfolk NR13 6HY (01603 270453 to book; www.broads-authority. gov.uk).* This electric boat carries visitors on tours of Malthouse Broad and also offers a ferry service between Ranworth Staithe and the Broads Wildlife Centre. *See* Places to Visit, page 91.

Liana (page 65) *Beccles Quay, Fen Lane, Beccles, Suffolk NR34 9QP (01502 713196; www.broads-authority.gov.uk).* An Edwardian-style electric launch which tours the River Waveney, giving visitors an opportunity to enjoy the beautiful scenery and wildlife.

Ra (page 43) *Gay's Staithe, Irstead Road, Neatishead, Norfolk NR12 8XP (01603 782281 to book; www.broads-authority. gov.uk).* A solar powered boat, named after the Egyptian sun god, takes visitors (including wheelchair users) around Barton Broad. *See also* Places to Visit, page 90.

The Norfolk Wildlife Trust runs regular trips by electric boat on Hickling Broad (page 40; *01692 598276 to book*) and Ranworth Broad (page 43; *01603 270479 to book*). *See also* Places to Visit, page 91.

NORFOLK WHERRIES

The Norfolk Wherry was a trading sailing craft which evolved to suit the particular conditions encountered on the Broads. It was highly manoeuvrable and could operate under most conditions. The mast was built to a special design, pivoting and counter-balanced by an enormous metal weight, which meant that it could be lowered quickly when passing under bridges. Cargoes of every description were carried in these boats until the building of railways and roads eclipsed their use.

Several wherries have been restored and are available for charter (*see* below). Each summer the Broads Authority offers a series of short sailing trips onboard a wherry. Contact any of the Broads Information Centres for details.

Norfolk Wherry Trust (page 44) *Forsythe Wherry Yard, Horsefen Road, Ludham, Norfolk NR29 5QG (01508 470992; www.wherryalbioncom).*

Norfolk Broads Yachting Company (page 43) *Southgate Yacht Station, Lower Street, Horning, Norwich, Norfolk NR12 8PF (01692 631330; www.norfolk-broads.com). See also* Where to Hire, page 72.

USING YOUR OWN CRAFT
Slipways and launch sites
There are public slipways at Beccles (page 65; *01502 712225*), Hickling Staithe (page 40), Horning (page 43; *01692 630434*), Horstead (page 42), Hoveton Riverside Park (page 42), Oulton Broad Yacht Station (*01502 574946*) and the Water Sports Centre (*01502 587163*)

both on page 67, Pug Lane Staithe at Repps with Bastwick (page 45), Smallburgh Staithe at Wayford Bridge (page 39), and Sutton Staithe (page 39). At the time of writing a new slipway is planned for Cantly (page 58).

Some boatyards have slipways which can be used for a small charge (a list is available from the Broads Authority and on its website). It is always advisable to telephone and confirm availability in advance.

Tolls and craft registration
Any vessel kept or used within the Broads Authority navigation area for more than 28 days must be registered with the Authority, carry third party insurance and have paid the appropriate annual toll. This applies to private craft, as all hire boats are registered with the Authority. Annual tolls can be paid through the Broads Authority main office.

Short visit tolls are available for periods of up to 28 days. All Broads Authority Information Centres and some yacht stations and boatyards issue short visit tolls. Craft registration is free and available from the Broads Authority main office, or visit their website.

Day boats for hire at Potter Heigham Staithe.

National Boat Safety Scheme

The Broads Authority operates the Boat Safety Scheme (BSS). This comprises essential safety requirements and is jointly managed by British Waterways and the Environment Agency, and administered through the Boat Safety Scheme office. Full information and *The Boat Safety Scheme Essential Guide* are available from the Broads Authority main office or direct from the Boat Safety Scheme, *64 Clarendon Road, Watford, Hertfordshire WD17 1DA (01923 201278; www.boatsafetyscheme.com)*. The website also offers useful advice on preventing fires and avoiding carbon monoxide poisoning.

A Boat Safety Certificate (for new boats, a Declaration of Conformity) is required by all craft with engines and/or with heating, lighting, cooking, refrigeration and other domestic appliances. It does not apply to open vessels solely propelled by an outboard motor as long as the vessel does not have any of the above facilities or appliances, and does not carry fuel other than that solely for use of powering the outboard motor.

Boats may visit the Broads navigation area for up to 28 days per year, on not more than four separate occasions, without the need to submit a valid BSS certificate to the Authority. Visiting boats will be subject to a random Dangerous Boat Check.

Traditional sailing boat on the Broads.

This chapter provides advice and information on various aspects of boating on the Broads. In all cases, further details and up-to-date lists of facilities can be obtained from the Broads Authority main office, their Information Centres and website. For contact details, *see* Where to Get More Information, page 24.

The Broads Authority have produced a film, *Better Boating on the Broads*, which contains lots of practical boat handling and navigation advice, as well as visitor and environmental information. It is particularly useful to those new to boating. The film is available to watch online (*www.broads-authority.gov.uk*) and to buy as a DVD (£1.50 including p&p at the time of writing) from the Broads Authority main office.

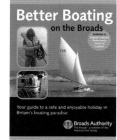

The *Boater's Handbook* is a booklet produced jointly by British Waterways and The Environment Agency and contains an introduction to basic boat handling and safety information. It is available to download free of charge from *www.britishwaterways.co.uk* and *www.environment-agency.gov.uk*.

BOAT HANDLING

If you are hiring a boat, your boatyard will brief you thoroughly on the various controls, boat handling and manoeuvring, and mooring. You will also be provided with a *Skipper's Guide* for ready reference while you are onboard.

- A cruiser is big and heavy and has no brakes. To stop it you must put it into reverse – it can take a long time to stop, so you must think and plan ahead.
- The water in a river or broad is always moving. The water and your boat will be affected by the winds and tides. Be aware that steering straight may not keep you on a straight path.
- Steering a boat with a rudder is different from steering a car. The boat pivots on its centre point and it is the bow (front) and the stern (back) of the boat that move. You will be facing the bow, but always think about what the back end of your boat is doing, to prevent it swinging out into other boats or the bank.
- Always manoeuvre the boat at slow speeds. You must be able to operate your boat without causing injury to people, wildlife, the environment, moorings, structures on the banks and other property.
- In general children under eight must not drive a motor boat. There are some circumstances in which children aged between eight and fourteen may drive a motor boat – visit *www.broads-authority.gov.uk* and check the Navigation Byelaws for details.
- Most boats turn better in one direction than another. When viewed from behind, most boats' propellers turn clockwise – these boats will turn better to port (left).

BOAT SAFETY SCHEME

See Getting Onto the Water, page 7.

Electric charging point.

Broads Authority Navigation Ranger.

BOATYARDS

Boatyards and other facilities are shown on the maps. Hire boaters should always contact their hire centre with any queries in the first instance.

BROADS AUTHORITY NAVIGATION RANGERS

The navigation rangers travel the Broads waterways in easily recognised boats. They enforce speed limits and carry out radar speed checks, and ensure that boats navigate properly. In addition, they are able to assist boaters with day-to-day issues including safety procedures, tidal conditions and planning.

BROADS RADIO CONTROL

Broads Radio Control deals with everything to do with navigating the Broads and rivers, from routine enquiries to emergency liaison with the coastguard, police and the Environment Agency. During peak season the office gets busy, so please be patient and do use the answerphone provided. In the event of an emergency, dial *999* – the emergency services will always contact Broads Control as required. Contact Broads Radio Control on *01603 756056* or *VHF channel 12*.

ELECTRIC CHARGING POINTS

There are 17 electric charging points throughout the Broads, on the rivers Ant, Bure, Chet, Thurne, Waveney, Wensum and Yare. They are indicated on the relevant mapping pages. The charging points not only enable electric boats to reliably travel throughout the Broads waterways, but allow the electricity supply on diesel powered boats to be topped up easily.

The charging pillars are straight forward to use and the charging cards are available from the Broads Authority head office, Broads Information Centres and other outlets close to the charging points.

EMERGENCIES

- Contact the emergency services by calling *999* for coastguard, fire, police or ambulance services.
- On a hire boat, contact details for your boatyard will be in your *Skipper's Handbook*.
- If you have to contact the emergency services or your boatyard, be as specific as possible about your location. Use the nearest Broads Authority 24 hour mooring as a reference to where you are – the name of the mooring is shown on

the signs. Always try to keep track of where you are on the Broads.
- Keep your mobile phone charged.
- Never enter the water, even in an emergency. Reach or throw but don't go into the water – reach with a broom, mop or towel, or throw a rope (keeping hold of one end), or anything that floats such as a life ring, ball or airtight container.
- *See also* Navigation Notes, page 14, and Stay Safe, page 18.

ENVIRONMENTALLY FRIENDLY BOATING

The Broads area is one of Europe's most important wetlands and conserving this beautiful but fragile environment is one of the responsibilities of the Broads Authority. As part of their work in sustainable tourism (recreation that does no lasting damage to the environment, or to people's enjoyment of it) the Authority actively promotes environmentally friendly boating.
- It is illegal to discharge sewage into the water of the Broads. Anyone doing so may be liable to a fine of up to £2,500. Facilities for pump out and sewage disposal are shown on the relevant map pages.
- Take extra care not to spill diesel into the water when refuelling. Spills of chemicals such as diesel cause harm to wildlife and can kill many water creatures. Spilling diesel or oil is a prosecutable offence.
- If you suspect an oil leak, do not pump out the bilges and release oil into the water. Instead, contact your boatyard immediately.
- If you see a pollution incident of any sort, telephone the Environment Agency free of charge on *0800 807060*, or Broads Radio Control on *01603 756056*.
- If you have your own boat, consider electric power. It is clean and convenient and there are charging points around the Broads (*see* Electric Charging Points, page 9). These charging points can also be used to charge on-board batteries: all you need is a cable with an appropriate socket to connect.

- All waste from boats, except sewage, empties straight into the river so that the cleaning products used have a direct impact on the environment. Reduce pollution by using biodegradable washing-up liquid and cleaning products, and try to use detergents containing no phosphate (also called sodium tripolyphosphate/STPP) or less then 5 per cent. Use only small amounts.
- Do not put cooking oil straight down the sink: absorb oil on to kitchen paper and put the paper in a bin. Oil can cause slicks on the water, causing particular problems for birds.
- Be careful with your rubbish. Discarded litter and fishing tackle can entangle and kill wildlife. Dispose of your rubbish carefully at proper sites. Do not leave bags of rubbish beside the bins, even if they are full – try to hold on to rubbish until you reach the next site. If there are problems with full bins, please contact the Broads Authority.

- Facilities for recycling and waste disposal are often available near moorings or in the local town or village. Details can be obtained from Broads Information Centres.
- Noise pollution should be avoided too. Be sensitive to your neighbours when moored up. Do not leave your engine idling late at night or early in the morning. Also be aware of the volume of your radio or television, particularly when the roof of your boat is down. Causing a noise nuisance could result in a fine of up to £1,000.
- If you have a dog with you, please clear up after it. Remember that although dogs are allowed on public rights of way, under close control, many nature reserves do not allow access for dogs.

- Keep an eye out for floating pennywort (*see* page 64). It was sold in this country as an ornamental plant for garden ponds, but it has escaped into the wild, where it stops native plants from growing and can cause serious problems for flood control and navigation. Do not let garden water plants get into the rivers and broads. If you think you have seen floating pennywort in the wild, please contact the Broads Authority or the Environment Agency.
- The Upper Thurne Broads (Hickling, Horsey and Martham) are internationally important for water birds. If you are there during the winter, please avoid the refuge areas (marked by buoys). Large flocks of ducks and geese spend the winter on the open water where they feed and roost and the refuges allow them to stay undisturbed.
- The Green Blue is an environmental awareness initiative supported by the British Marine Federation and the Royal Yachting Association, for those in the marine business and all those who enjoy boating and watersports. Visit *www.thegreenblue.org.uk* for lots of practical advice and information.

FUEL

Hire craft usually carry fuel sufficient for the rental period. Many boatyards will include the cost of fuel in the hire price. If you are charged, it will only be for the fuel used, and this will be deducted from your fuel deposit when you return the boat. The *Skipper's Notes* will include more details. Fuel outlets are marked on the map pages.

GOING AGROUND

The Broads is an area of tidal waterways and the tidal effect will be most strongly felt in the Breydon Water area and the lower reaches of the southern rivers. Water levels rise and fall depending upon the state of the tide. It is important to always stay within any channel marking posts. Should you go aground, try reversing gently, or pushing off with the boat hook. Another method is to get your crew to rock the boat from side to side using the boat

hook, or move all crew to the end opposite to that which is aground. If you have any problems, contact your boatyard or telephone Broads Radio Control on *01603 756056*.

LAVATORIES

Hire craft are usually fitted with flushing, sealed unit toilets. They are emptied via a process called 'pump out', which is simple and clean and carried out at boatyards and yacht stations. Pump out facilities are shown on the map pages. Have the toilets pumped out before things become critical. If you are hiring your craft, check the *Skipper's Notes* for more information.

MOORING

Free moorings are available at many locations in the Broads for a maximum stay of 24 hours. These moorings can be used by all boats, and many of them can also be used by anglers. There are also moorings available at public staithes, pubs and boatyards, although there may be a charge to use these.

Mooring up and casting off can be one of the most difficult parts of handling a boat, but with preparation and a little practice you will soon be confident. Plan ahead – make sure that your ropes are ready and that your crew knows what to do. The fittest adult (not a child) should always step (not jump!) ashore and should wear a life-jacket.

- If the mooring is staffed, please follow all directions given by the rangers.
- Always approach a mooring against the tide, with a careful hand on the throttle. You will be able to to hold the boat stationary heading into the tide and approach the mooring sideways under control.
- Always drop your mud weight when moored, especially if mooring stern on (the back of the boat), when the mud weight will stop the bow (the front) swinging around.
- Allow slack in mooring ropes to allow for rises and falls in the water level as the tides rise and fall – check your mooring ropes regularly.

Moored boats at Upton Dyke (page 53).

- Do not trail mooring ropes across footpaths and never run alongside moorings, to avoid tripping on ropes or posts.

REGATTAS

Regattas, organised by sailing, power boat and rowing clubs, are very much part of the boating heritage of the Broads. They can be great fun for spectators as well as the participants – bridges are often a good vantage point. Regular events take place each year and details are available from the Broads Information Centres and the Norfolk and Suffolk Boating Association (*www.thegreenbook.org.uk*). If you find yourself on the water during a regatta:

- Keep close to the right hand bank.
- Sailing boats have right of way. Slow down and try to pass behind them.
- Make your course clear – do not weave about.
- Watch for any indications by the crew as to when they would like you to pass, but do not put yourself or others in danger.
- In some areas particular channels may be provided for your safe passage. In these cases stay within the channel. During powerboat racing, do not enter or leave via the body of the broad where the event is taking place.

- Listen carefully to any advice, and follow any guidance from navigation rangers or safety patrol boats.

SLIPWAYS

See Getting Onto the Water, page 6.

SPEED LIMITS

There are speed limits of 3, 4, 5 or 6 mph in force throughout the Broads waterways. The limits are in place to reduce erosion of the river banks, prevent disturbance to water-level nesting birds, and protect people on moored boats. They are clearly signed on the riverbanks and are enforced by the navigation rangers. There is no need to go any faster – the faster you go, the bigger a wave (wash) the boat creates: if your wash is breaking against the bank, causing large waves or throwing moored boats around, slow down. Even if you are under the speed limit, you may still be fined if you are creating excess wash, so check it regularly, especially if you are on a day boat or just getting used to the speed of your boat at the start of a holiday. Slow down also when passing engineering works and anglers, when there is a lot of floating rubbish on the water (try to drift over obvious obstructions in neutral), when approaching blind corners, bridges and junctions. Remember that if your boat is moving in the same direction as the tide, your speed will be faster than indicated.

TIDE TABLES

Tide tables are available from Broads Authority Information Centres and *www.broads-authority.gov.uk*. Local newspapers also publish tide times and the BBC website lists them, at *www.bbc.co.uk/weather/coast*.

TOLLS AND REGISTRATION

See Getting onto the Water, page 6.

WATER

Hire boats will have a full tank of water for drinking and washing. You should top up your water regularly. Water points are indicated on the map pages. If you are hiring a boat, check the *Skipper's Notes* for more information.

WATER SKIING

Water skiing has been a regular Broads activity since 1951. Today there are ten allocated ski runs on the rivers Waveney and Yare. Water skiing may only take place at certain times and all skiers must be members of the Eastern Rivers Water Ski Club and British Water Ski. More information, including the times water skiing is permitted, is available from the Easter Rivers Water Ski club website at *www.erwsc.co.uk*.

- Boat owners must obtain a skiing permit from the Broads Authority.
- All boat drivers must have passed the Sports Boat Drivers Award.
- All boats must have British Water Ski approved public liability insurance.
- Each of the water skiing zones on the Broads is clearly sign-posted. If you cruise through one of the water ski areas you must proceed cautiously as there may be skiers in the water.
- Keep to the right hand side of the river wherever possible.
- Keep a constant speed and course. Stop only to avoid collision or a skier in the water. Ski boats are fast and manoeuvrable and will keep out of your way.
- A yellow flag will be flown by all ski boats when skiing is underway. On seeing the flag, slow down, give the ski boat a wide berth and keep an extra look out for skiers in the water.

WEIL'S DISEASE

See Stay Safe, page 19.

Water skiing on the Broads.

NAVIGATION NOTES

The Broads are generally a safe and trouble free environment for boating, which is why they are so popular with all boaters, from the experienced to those hiring a boat for the first time. This chapter highlights issues you need to be aware of in advance of your boat trip and provides you with information to help you navigate the Broads waters safely and enjoyably.

ACCIDENTS

If someone is injured or there is serious damage to your boat, or to someone else's, you must stop as soon as is practicable.

- You must inform Broads Radio Control of the incident *(01603 756056)* and give the name and address of the boat owner, and the boat registration number.
- You must also give this information to anyone else who has good reason to request it.
- Hire boaters must also inform their hire centre and there will be instructions on what to do in the *Skipper's Guide*.
- If you have an accident where property is damaged but no one is injured, you must stop your boat and give your name and address, that of the boat owner and the boat registration number, to anyone who has good reason to need it.
- You should take all reasonable steps to find out who the damaged property or boat belongs to, let them know in writing what has happened and give your name and address.
- Complete an Incident Report Form, which you can get from a boatyard, the Broads Authority, their Information Centres or website.
- You may be liable to a fine of up to £1,000 if you do not follow these procedures.

BRIDGES

Bridges can be fixed or moveable. Bridge heights shown on the maps are for central clearance at high water on a normal tide. River levels vary considerably, depending upon weather conditions and the tide, and can affect the figures given.

- There is a gauge board on either side of the approach to most bridges, which will give you the current clearance available. Check this carefully to ensure that you have clearance. *See also* page 30.
- The air draft is the height of your boat from the waterline to the highest part of the boat (shown on a plate in the cockpit of hire boats).
- Think ahead when approaching all bridges. Lower the canopy and/or windscreen. Get everyone off the deck. Ensure that all hands and heads are in board in plenty of time before the bridge.
- Never race for a bridge or try to hurry through. Consider moored boats and monitor your boat wash. Keep to the speed limits.
- Watch for other boats coming through. Generally the boat travelling with the current has right of way.
- Don't raise your head until you are well clear of the bridge and **never** try to fend off using hands or feet.
- Yachts will need to lower their masts at all bridges except Reedham, Somerleyton and Trowse swing bridges and the lifting bridges on Breydon Water, and Novi Sad and Carrow Road bridges in Norwich.

Children should wear life-jackets at all times, on the water and beside it.

- At Potter Heigham you must use the bridge pilot to take you through, available 08.30–18.00, depending on tide and weather conditions. *Telephone 01692 670460.*
- At Wroxham there is an optional bridge pilot available to help you. Some hire boatyards insist that their customers use the service – check with the boatyard or look in the *Skipper's Manual*. The service is available 09.00–17.00. *Telephone 01603 783043.*
- If you have any problems, telephone Broads Radio Control on *01603 756056.*

Moveable bridges
- At lift and swing bridges, a single red flag indicates the bridge is working and in service; two red flags indicate that the bridge is not working and not in service.
- Bridges will only open for craft clearly unable to pass under (i.e. if you need to lower a canopy or windscreen, you must do so).
- The signal requiring the bridge to open is three prolonged blasts on the horn or whistle.
- Most bridges monitor *VHF channel 12*. The radio will not be answered during emergency matters relating to the rail network.

GREAT YARMOUTH AND BREYDON WATER
You will have to pass through Great Yarmouth and across Breydon Water if you want to cruise between the northern rivers (Bure, Ant and Thurne) and the southern rivers (Yare, Chet and Waveney). This requires careful thought and forward planning.

Great Yarmouth
(*see* Breydon Bridge inset, page 68)
- You must time your arrival in Great Yarmouth to coincide with slack low water or just afterwards. Slack low water is around $1\frac{1}{4}$ hours after low water at Great Yarmouth Yacht Station. Check a tide table to find out when this is. At slack low water the current is weaker, so it is easier to moor, and there is more

room under the bridges. At high water you will not be able to get under the bridges, and there is nowhere safe to moor to wait for the tide to drop on the Breydon Water side.
- It takes around $2\frac{1}{4}$ hours to travel from Acle to Great Yarmouth, and about 2 hours from Reedham or St Olaves. *See* page 31 for journey times.
- Check the map and follow the directions. The water is shallow outside the posted channel so it is important to keep within the posts.
- You may wait free of charge at Great Yarmouth Yacht Station while the tide drops to allow safe passage under the bridges.
- Always approach the moorings against the tide.
- It may be difficult to turn in the narrow river, so turn well upstream or down, depending on the tide, giving yourself plenty of time.
- If the river is busy, be prepared to go down through the bridges and turn where there is more room.
- You must not proceed downstream if three vertical red lights are on the Yarmouth/Acle Road Bridge.

Breydon Water
(*see* South Breydon Water inset, page 69)
- The Broads Authority operate a navigation ranger patrol in the Breydon Water area.
- In high winds and at high tide, Breydon Water can be rough. Crossing at the right time, at low water, should avoid this problem.
- Everyone should wear a life-jacket when crossing Breydon Water.
- Do not navigate Breydon Water (or anywhere else) in fog.
- The Broads Authority have free 24 hour moorings between the Berney Arms pub and the wind pump (mill). Use them to wait for favourable tides to cross Breydon Water.
- For advice on whether or not to cross, contact your boatyard or telephone Broads Radio Control on *01603 756056.*

Navigation Notes

INCIDENT REPORTING

Incident Report Forms are obtainable from the Broads Authority, their Information Centres and website, and boatyards. Use the form to report any accident, incident or near miss that you witness or are involved in. The form can also be used to report any incidence of vandalism or threatening behaviour, but please do not use the form in place of reporting incidents to the police. *See also* Accidents, page 14, and Police, page 19.

NAVIGATION ADVICE

Ask any navigation ranger or quay ranger, or telephone Broads Radio Control on *01603 756056*. The Broads Authority publish *Waterways Code* leaflets covering such subjects as safety and mooring. The leaflets are available from the Authority and their Information Centres, and can also be downloaded from their website.

NOTICE TO MARINERS

A Notice to Mariners is required whenever any work is undertaken that may significantly affect the navigation, such as river and bridge closures, bridge opening times and special events. The Broads Authority publish the Notices on their website.

RULES OF THE ROAD

- Keep your boat close to the right hand bank.
- Sailing boats have right of way over motor boats. Slow down and try to pass behind them.
- Make your course clear – do not weave about or try to stop suddenly.
- Watch for any indications by other crews as to when they would like you to pass, but do not put yourself or others in danger.
- In some areas particular channels may be provided for your safe passage. In these cases, stay within the channel. During powerboat racing, do not enter or leave via the body of the broad where the racing is taking place.

*St Benet's Abbey, most easily accessed by boat (*see *Places to Visit, page 87).*

- Listen carefully to, and take any guidance from navigation rangers or safety patrol boats.
- Keep clear of commercial traffic and watch for any instructions from their crew.
- Keep clear of craft under tow.
- Do not exceed the speed limits.
- Navigation lights are required after dark. (Generally, hire boats may not travel after dark.)
- On the River Yare you may meet coasters travelling between Cantley and Great Yarmouth. They will be escorted by Broads Authority navigation rangers and it is important that you follow their directions.
- You must not fish from a motor or sailing boat which is underway.

SAFE NAVIGATING

- Over the next 20 years or so Edmund Nuttall contractors will be working on flood defences throughout the Broads, which will necessitate moving heavy plant and equipment around the waterways. Take note of warning signs and keep clear of the machinery.
- On the western (railway) side of Haddiscoe Cut (page 59), avoid the gabion wire baskets, containing flints. They are there to help build up the flood banks. Stay within the marked posts. Take care when mooring in this area after works have been completed, until the new banks are established.
- A chain-operated ferry operates at Reedham (page 59). Particular care must be taken when it is in operation. Wait until the ferry has docked before passing, to avoid catching the chains with your propeller, and be ready to obey any instruction from the ferry operator.

URGENT BOATING NEWS/ URGENT ENVIRONMENTAL NEWS

You will find these two items on the Broads Authority website. The pages highlight important boating, environmental and safety matters.

Norwich Castle Museum and Art Gallery. (see Places to Visit, page 86).

Boating is a safe pastime. However, it makes sense to take some simple safety precautions. The following notes offer advice to keep you safe during your time on the Broads.

COOKING OUTDOORS

- Do not use barbecues on your boat.
- Keep them away from fuel.
- Do not place them on anything which will burn.
- Do not put them where people will be walking.
- Dispose of them carefully in a bin or skip only when fully extinguished.

DOGS

Dogs tend to fall overboard quite regularly and are just as susceptible to cold and other water hazards. Keep them safe too. You can buy life-jackets for them as well! Remember that you should never enter the water to rescue a pet – you would be putting your own life at risk.

DON'T JUMP!

The majority of injuries occur through jumping on or off a boat. Step carefully and keep a good handhold.

FIRE SAFETY

Sadly, fire-related accidents and injuries occur on boats every year. Fire can spread quickly on a boat, even on the water, so follow safety precautions and be prepared.

- Be careful with naked flames and never leave the boat with the hob or oven lit. Turn things off until you come back to the boat.
- Familiarise yourself and your crew with the locations and operation of the fire extinguishers. If you are hiring a boat, this should be covered in the boatyard handover and in the *Skipper's Manual*.
- Never block ventilation grills. Boats are enclosed spaces and levels of carbon monoxide can build up from faulty appliances or just from using the cooker.
- If you own your own craft, consider

fitting alarms and detectors to help keep you and your crew safe.

- Extinguish all naked flames before refuelling. Turn off the engine and cooker before handling any fuel. Never smoke when refuelling or changing a gas cylinder.
- If in doubt, do not fight a fire yourself. Get out, stay out and wait for the emergency services.
- Visit *www.direct.gov.uk* or follow the link from the Broads Authority website (go to Boating Safety Tips and Contacts) for a useful leaflet containing advice on avoiding fires aboard.

HANDS AND FEET ARE PRECIOUS

Never try to stop your boat or fend off with your hands or feet. Your hands and feet are much more precious than any boat or structure. Always keep hands and feet inside the boat.

KEEP AN EYE ON YOUR CREW

It is important to know where your crew is at all times. It is possible for people, especially children, to fall overboard without anyone noticing. Do not let children sit on the front of the boat, or play at the stern or on the roof unsupervised, especially when the boat is underway.

LIFE-JACKETS

It is advisable to wear a life-jacket on deck at all times, even if you can swim. Children, the less mobile, and the elderly should always wear a life-jacket, even when the boat is moored. The water is very cold at all times of the year, and even strong swimmers can get into trouble quickly.

MIND YOUR HEAD

Take great care when going through bridges. Make sure that everyone is inside the boat and off the deck, and that all heads and hands are inboard in plenty of time before the bridge. Do not raise your head until you are well past the bridge.

NO SWIMMING

Never swim in the Broads. The water may look inviting, but it is a natural, wild place and always cold, no matter what the time of year or temperature. The cold shock of entering the water can kill. With your head just above water, you are nearly invisible to boaters. There are lots of hazards underwater such as weed, obstacles, fast currents and the naturally occurring, but poisonous blue-green algae. Areas particularly susceptible to blue-green algae include Barton, Ranworth, South Walsham, Thurne and Whitlingham. *See also* information on Weil's Disease below.

POLICE

The Broads has its own dedicated police officers – the Broads Beat. For non-urgent matters, telephone *0845 4564567* and ask for the Broads Beat. In any emergency, always telephone *999*.

REVERSING

Never approach anyone in the water stern (the back of the boat) first. The propeller is located at the stern and will seriously injure anyone in the water.

SPEED AND WASH

See Boating Need to Know, page 12.

STEADY WITH THE DRINK

Relaxing with an alcoholic drink is a pleasant part of a holiday for many people. But, it is essential to keep your wits about you while on the water. It is recommended that the helmsman does not drink until the boat is moored for the night. You can be fined for navigating while not being in proper control of your boat – either through drinking or drug use. Getting on and off the boat, and moving around the deck, during the day and more particularly at night, can be hazardous when you have had a few drinks – you are more likely to fall in, and your chances of survival are reduced.

REFUELLING

- Always switch off your engine and clean up any spillage.
- Do not refuel a boat while underway.
- Fill petrol cans away from the boat – do not refuel the motor directly.
- Petrol must be stored in a low risk position, in compliance with current regulations (available from the Broads Authority).
- Extinguish all naked lights (including pilot lights on fridges, etc) during refuelling.
- Hot surfaces can present a hazard.
- Hire boaters should refer to their *Skipper's Manual* for instructions.

SAFETY ON AND OFF THE WATER

Be very careful alongside water, not just when you are on a boat.

- It is advisable to wear a life-jacket when boarding a boat and getting ashore. Children, weak swimmers, the less mobile and the elderly should wear a life-jacket anywhere near the water's edge.
- Wear suitable clothing and sensible shoes. Check out the weather forecast so that you are prepared.
- Take a torch if you will be returning to your boat after dark.
- When you go ashore, take careful note of your surroundings and any possible hazards. Plan a safe route back to your boat.
- Consider always returning to your boat with a companion, especially if returning late at night.

WEIL'S DISEASE

Weil's disease is a potentially serious, and even fatal condition, which can be contracted from rivers and other water sources, through cuts and scratches. Always wash your hands after contact with the water. If you fall in, wash yourself thoroughly, or shower, and wash your wet clothes before wearing them again. Clean cuts and scratches with an antiseptic and protect them with a plaster. The infection may seem like flu in the early stages and can occur two–four weeks after exposure. If you experience any flu-like symptoms after contact with the water, get medical advice immediately and mention the possibility of Weil's disease – not all medical practitioners will immediately consider it. More information is available from *www.leptospirosis.org*.

Although boating is one of the best ways to enjoy the Broads, there are plenty of opportunities for other activities throughout the area.

ACCESS FOR ALL

Access for everyone is increasing throughout the Broads all the time, from wheelchair accessible boats (for short trips and holidays), to facilities to help people with visual or hearing impairments. For details of wheelchair-friendly hire available, *see* Where to Hire, page 70.

Boardwalks, suitable for wheelchairs and pushchairs, allow everyone to visit the mysterious and swampy woodlands around many of the broads. A list of accessible boardwalks can be found in the Walking section, *see* page 22. For anglers, details of wheelchair accessible fishing platforms may be found under Angling, below. And, for cyclists, one of the Broads cycle hire centres has electric bikes available for hire (*see* Cycling, below).

In the chapter on Places to Visit (*see* page 86), we have tried, as far as possible, to note where there is wheelchair access and disabled toilet facilities, and for the nature reserves, to give an indication of accessibility.

The Broads Authority, Broads Information Centres (all have wheelchair access and induction loop systems, although access is limited at Potter Heigham and Toad Hole Cottage) and Tourist Information Centres can provide more help. The Broads Authority website contains much information on access, including a list of accessible toilets. The Authority's annual visitor magazine, *Broadcaster*, is available in a large print version and on audio tape. Contact the Broads Authority or their Information Centres for more details.

For other contacts, *see* Where to Get More Information, page 24.

ANGLING

The Broads is one of the country's best-known fishing areas, supporting a diversity of species, such as bream, eel, perch, pike, roach, rudd and tench. The coarse fishing season runs from mid-June to mid-March. You will need a current Environment Agency licence, available from post offices. Regular fishing matches take place throughout the area. Some local anglers offer tuition days. Contact the Broads Authority for details or take a look through *Angle on the Broads* (*see* below).

There are many places to fish from the bank or hire a day boat (*see* Where to Hire, page 70). Fishing platforms suitable for wheelchair users can be found at Rollesby Bridge (page 45), Filby Broad (pages 45–6), Potter Heigham (on the south bank, page

An angler fishing from the bank.

Cyclists on Ludham Bridge.

45), along the River Bure near Cockshoot Broad (page 43; for members of the Norwich and District Anglers' Association; *01603 423625; www.ndaa.org.uk*) and at Martham Pits (page 45; Martham and District Angling Club; *01493 748358*).

The Broads waterways have been strongly associated with pike fishing for many years, and the thought of catching a specimen pike is often a lure for holiday anglers. Pike fossils found in Norfolk date from more than half-a-million years ago and the fish has been hunted in the Broads over hundreds of years, for food and, more recently, for sport. *Angle on the Broads* includes detailed advice on how to catch a pike.

- Never discard fishing tackle, especially baited hooks.
- It is an offence to leave a baited rod unattended. As well as the danger from passing boats, it is potentially hazardous to water birds and fish.
- Watch out for birds swimming into your line. Swans can reach bait deep below the water's surface and other birds will dive for food – wind in your tackle if you think that birds might be at risk.
- Try to ensure that you are visible to approaching boats and acknowledge a boat helm's efforts to keep out of your way.

- If you are fishing from a Broads Authority free mooring, you must give way to boats wishing to moor.
- Fish should be returned to the water quickly and gently after weighing (if this is necessary) or after being retained in a keep net. Only use a keep net where necessary and retain fish for the shortest possible time.
- Do not fish from a moving boat. Always wear a life-jacket when fishing from any craft.
- *Angle on the Broads* is a guide published for anglers, containing comprehensive information on fishing on the Broads, including locations for free bank fishing, and details of fishing boat hire and fishing tackle shops. It is available from Broads Information Centres or from the Broads Authority website.

CYCLING

It is fun to explore the Broads by bike, whether you want an easy, family-friendly short route, or something longer and more demanding. There are miles of quiet country lanes, a great choice of bike trails and several Sustrans traffic-free routes through the area.

There is a network of cycle hire centres (*see* Where to Hire, page 70) from where bikes can be hired by the day or half-day,

21

and free cycle route maps are available. Most centres have tandems and the hire centre at Ludham Bridge (page 44) has two electric bikes, suitable for people with limited mobility.

The Bike Hire Association has created nine circular rides ranging from between 9 km (5.5 miles) to almost 37 km (23 miles) which explore the northern Broads area, and include links to off-road routes and a boundary route of 93 km (58 miles). These routes pass interesting places to visit and refreshment stops. You'll enjoy wonderful views of the surrounding countryside and the lakes and rivers. Route 5 takes in the Norfolk coast between Somerton and Sea Palling (page 40), offering opportunities to explore the beaches.

There is also a Broadland Churches Trail, a circular route of 56 km (35 miles), with shorter options, that takes in 16 beautiful Broadland churches from Hoveton (page 42) to Horning (page 43), via Wroxham, Ranworth, South Walsham and Acle.

The South Trinity Broads Benefice Cycle Trail, another circular route, comprises 20 km (12.5 miles) of easy cycling (with a shorter option), visiting seven special ancient Broads churches. It starts from Filby (page 46) and continues on through Thrigby, Mautby, Runham, Stokesby, Billockby and Fleggburgh (page 45).

The Bure Valley Path is a 14.5 km (9 mile) scenic railway path, for walkers and cyclists, which runs between Aylsham and Wroxham (page 42).

Details of all these routes are available from the cycle hire centres, the Broads Authority and their Information Centres, or visit *www.thebroadsbybike.org.uk* for routes and maps. Norfolk County Council also offers cycle routes on its countryside website (*www.countrysideaccess.norfolk. gov.uk*), as does Suffolk County Council's countryside website (*www.discoversuffolk. org.uk*), where you will find a wide range of short and long distance cycle routes.

Sustrans National Cycle Routes (NCR) 1 and 13, and Regional Route 30 pass through Norfolk. For details of these, Norwich city cycle routes and free cycling maps, visit *www.sustrans.org.uk*.

The Sustrans routes through Suffolk are NCR 1 and 51, and Regional Routes 30 and 41. Again, visit the Sustrans website for full details of these routes and cycle maps for Lowestoft and Beccles.

WALKING

There are more than 306 km (190 miles) of footpaths throughout the Broads, including nature trails, circular walks and long distance footpaths. Remember that dogs are allowed on public rights of way under close control, but many nature reserves do not allow access for dogs.

Broads Walks comprise a collection of short strolls and longer hikes throughout the area, offering opportunities to enjoy each of the Broads rivers. For example, you could take a 4.5 km (3 mile) circular stroll from Irstead Staithe (page 44), or

explore the Beccles Marshes (page 65) along a 6.5 km (4 mile) trail. Leaflets of all the walks are available from the Broads Authority and their Information Centres, or visit the website and download route maps.

There are two series of Broads Walks along public footpaths: the Bure Valley Walks (at Cockshoot, Filby, Oby, Salhouse, Stokesby, Tunstall, Upton and West Caister); and the Waveney Valley Walks (Beccles, Bungay, Burgh Castle, Carlton Marshes, Geldeston, Gillingham and Haddiscoe). Packs containing directions and maps for the walks are available from Broads Authority Information Centres.

Three waymarked long distance footpaths run through the Broads. The Weavers' Way (from Cromer on the north Norfolk coast to Great Yarmouth, page 55) and the Angles Way (from Great Yarmouth to Knettishall Heath Country Park in Breckland, via the Waveney and Little Ouse valleys) are detailed on *www.countrysideaccess.norfolk.gov.uk*, where you can get more information and download route maps. The Wherryman's

Way follows the River Yare between Norwich (page 49) and Great Yarmouth (page 55). Visit *www.wherrymansway.net* for lots of useful information, circular walks, access details and descriptions of local heritage highlights passed en route.

For more walks in the southern part of the Broads, visit Suffolk County Council's countryside website *www.discoversuffolk.org.uk* which offers routes for a wide range of walks together with details of the several long distance routes through the area.

Boardwalks and easy access paths suitable for wheelchair users can be found at the following Broads locations:

Beccles Marsh Trails (page 65), Chedgrave (page 57), Filby Broad (page 54), Horsey Mere (page 41), Horstead Mill (page 42), Hoveton Riverside Park (page 42), Rockland St Mary (page 57), Salhouse Broad (page 43), Whitlingham Country Park (page 50); and on nature reserves at Barton Broad (page 39), Carlton Marshes (page 66), Cockshoot Broad (page 43), Hickling Broad (page 40), Ranworth Broad (page 43) and Wheatfen (page 57).

Poppies in a Norfolk field.

This chapter contains contact details and weblinks to help you plan your visit and for when you are in the area. We have included all sorts of different organisations, from the Broads Authority itself to all those others who can provide information and/or services to help make your visit to the area more enjoyable.

The Broads Authority

(*see* Norwich inset map, page 48)
Dragonfly House, 2 Gilders Way, Norwich, Norfolk NR3 1UB; 01603 610734; email broads@broads-authority.gov.uk; www.broads-authority.gov.uk; www.enjoythebroads.com.

BROADS INFORMATION CENTRES

Knowledgeable staff and the information on offer will help you make the most of your visit to the Broads. The centres are open seasonally. During the winter, contact the Broads Authority offices in Norwich.

Beccles

The Quay, Fen Lane, Beccles, Suffolk NR34 9BH (01603 756093; email becclestic@broads-authority.gov.uk). Open Easter–May and Oct, Mon–Fri 09.00–13.00 and 14.00–17.00; Sat–Sun 09.00–17.00. Jun–Sep and end Oct, daily 09.00–17.00.

Hoveton/Wroxham

Station Road, Hoveton, Norwich, Norfolk NR12 8UR (01603 756097; email hovetontic@broads-authority.gov.uk). Open Easter–Oct, daily 09.00–13.00 and 13.30–17.00.

How Hill

Toad Hole Cottage Museum, How Hill, Ludham, Great Yarmouth, Norfolk NR29 5PG (01603 756096; email toadholetic@broads-authority.gov.uk). Open Easter–May and Oct, Mon–Fri 10.30–13.00 and 13.30–15.00; Sat–Sun 10.30–17.00. Jun–Sep, daily 09.30–18.00.

Potter Heigham

The Staithe, Bridge Road, Potter Heigham, Norfolk NR29 5JD (01603 756098; email potterheighamtic@broads-authority.gov.uk). Open Easter–Oct, daily 09.00–13.00 and 13.30–17.00.

Ranworth

The Staithe, Farm Lane, Norwich, Norfolk NR13 6HY (01603 756095; email ranworthtic@broads-authority.gov.uk). Open Easter–Oct, daily 09.00–17.00.

Whitlingham Visitor Centre

Whitlingham Lane, near Trowse, Norwich, Norfolk NR14 8TR (01603 756094; email whitlinghamtic@broads-authority.gov.uk). Open Easter–Oct, daily 10.00–14.00 and 14.30–16.00 (closes 17.00 during school holidays).

The Broads Authority produces an annual visitor magazine, *Broadcaster*, which contains a lot of information on places to stay, things to do and a full events listing. It is available from the Broads Authority and their Information Centres.

TOURIST INFORMATION CENTRES

Open all year.

East of England Tourism

Dettingen House, Dettingen Way, Bury St Edmunds, Suffolk IP33 3TU (01284 727470; email info@eet.org.uk; www.visiteastofengland.com).

Aylsham

Bure Valley Railway Station, Norwich Road, Aylsham, Norfolk NR11 6BW (01263 733903; email aylsham.tic@ broadland.gov.uk).

Great Yarmouth

25 Marine Parade, Great Yarmouth, Norfolk NR30 2EW (01493 846345; email tourism@great-yarmouth.gov.uk; www.great-yarmouth.co.uk).

Lowestoft
East Point Pavilion, Royal Plain, Lowestoft, Suffolk NR33 0AP (01502 533600; email touristinfo@waveney.gov.uk; www.visit-lowestoft.co.uk).

Norwich
The Forum, Millennium Plain, Norwich, Norfolk NR2 1TF (01603 213999; email tourism@norwich.gov.uk; www.visitnorwich.co.uk).

MORE WEBSITES FOR VISITORS TO THE BROADS
Discover the Broads, a guide to 12 great days out in the Broads, compiled by people who live there *www.discoverthebroads.com.*

Guide for Norwich, South Norfolk and Broadland *www.visitnorwich.co.uk.*

Norfolk Broads, a non-commercial website with lots of information and photos *www.norfolk-broads.org.*

Norfolk County Council *www.norfolk.gov.uk.*

Norfolk County Council's countryside website *www.countrysideaccess.norfolk.gov.uk.*

Norfolk Tourism *www.visitnorfolk.gov.uk.*

Norfolk Tourist Attractions Association *www.norfolktouristattractions.co.uk.*

Norfolk Windmills Trust. Contact for details about mill open days *01603 222705; www.norfolkwindmills.co.uk.*

South Norfolk Council and the Arts Council England, promoting places to visit, things to do, places to stay and cultural events of all types throughout the southern Broads *www.southernbroads.com.*

Suffolk County Council *www.suffolk.gov.uk.*

Suffolk County Council's countryside website *www.discoversuffolk.org.uk.*

Suffolk Tourism *www.visit-suffolk.org.uk.*

OTHER USEFUL CONTACTS

ACCESS FOR ALL
Dial UK (Disability Information Advice Line) *telephone 01302 310123; fax 01302 310404; textphone 01302 310123; email enquiries@dialuk.org.uk; www.dialuk.org.uk.*

Disability Rights Commission Helpline *telephone 08457 622633; fax 08457 778878; textphone 08457 62644; www.drc-gb.org.*

NDIS (Norfolk Disability Information Service) *telephone 01603 729802; fax 01603 729809; www.getphysical.norfolk.gov.uk.*

RADAR (Royal Association for Disability and Rehabilition) *telephone 020 7250 3222; fax 020 7250 0212; minicom 020 7250 4119; email radar@radar.org.uk; www.radar.org.uk.*

Tourism for All (the UK voice for accessible tourism) *telephone 0845 124 9971; fax 01539 735567; minicom 0845 124 9976; www.tourismforall.org.uk.*

ANGLING
Martham and District Angling Club *01493 748358*

Norwich and District Anglers' Association *01603 423625; www.ndaa.org.uk.*

BOATING
For boatyards, hire centres and booking agencies, *see* Where to Hire, page 70.

Bridge Pilots: Potter Heigham *01692 670460;* Wroxham *01603 783043.*

British Waterways, responsible for maintaining many of the country's canals and inland waterways *0845 6715530; www.britishwaterways.co.uk.*

British Waterways' leisure website *0845 6715530; www.waterscape.com.*

Boat Safety Scheme *01923 201278;*
www.boatsafetyscheme.com.

Broads Radio Control, for advice and
assistance with navigation on the Broads
01603 756056; VHF channel 12.

Community boating associations,
encouraging more people to access the
waterways – for individuals, young people,
disabled and other community groups
0845 0510649; www.national-cba.co.uk.

Environment Agency, manages around
966 km (600 miles) of the country's rivers
08708 506 506;
www.environment-agency.gov.uk.

Inland Waterways Association,
campaigning for the conservation, use,
maintenance, restoration and
development of Britain's inland waterways
01494 783453; www.waterways.org.uk.

Norfolk and Suffolk Boating Association.
The website includes an events
programme *www.thegreenbook.org.uk.*

Royal Yachting Association (RYA). The
national body for all forms of boating;
administers accredited courses for all
types of craft. *02380 604100;*
www.rya.org.uk.

The Green Blue, promoting sustainable use
of coastal and inland waters
www.thegreenblue.org.uk.

UK waterways: non-commercial, with more
than 2,000 links to canal and waterways
related websites *www.canals.com.*

BRIDGE PILOTS *See* Boating, page 25.

CANOEING
British Canoe Union, the UK's governing
body for the sport *0845 370 9500;*
www.bcu.org.uk.

CYCLING
Cycle routes in the Broads
www.thebroadsbybike.org.uk.

CTC, the UK's National Cyclists'
Organisation *0844 736 8450;*
www.ctc.org.uk.

For those who like to cycle with a GPS
device: lots of routes to share at
www.gps-routes.co.uk.

Sustrans, the UK's leading sustainable
transport charity *0845 113 0065;*
www.sustrans.org.uk.

CHURCH SERVICES
Churches together on the Broads
0790 572149;
www.churchestogetheronthebroads.org.uk.

HEALTH
NHS Direct *0845 46 47;*
www.nhsdirect.nhs.uk.

Norfolk and Norwich University Hospital
(Norwich) *01603 286286;*
www.nnuh.nhs.uk.

James Paget Hospital (Great Yarmouth)
01493 452452; www.jpaget.nhs.uk.

NATIONAL PARKS
There are 14 members of the National
Parks family, including the Broads
029 2049 9966; www.nationalparks.org.

NON-NATIVE SPECIES
The GB Non-Native Species Secretariat.
Detailed information and recognition
guides *www.nonnativespecies.org.*

POLICE
Telephone *999* in emergencies. The Broads
also has its own dedicated police officers.
For non-urgent matters, telephone
0845 4564567 and ask for the
Broads Beat.

POLLUTION
For any pollution incident, telephone
Broads Radio Control on *01603 756056*
(during the day) or the Environment
Agency on *0800 807060.* For serious
pollution incidents outside office hours,
contact the coastguard on *999.*

RADIO CONTROL
See Boating Need to Know, page 9.

TRAVEL
The First number 12 bus offers a service (Mon–Sat) from Norwich, taking in a picturesque route through Rackheath, Hoveton, Horning, Ludham and Catfield to Stalham *08456 020 121* or contact Traveline (*see* below).

The Acle area Flexibus serves many Broads villages. It is operated by OURBUS as a demand responsive service – book in advance *01493 752223*.

From Norwich the Bittern railway line (*www.bitternline.com*) goes north through Wroxham; the Wherry line (*www.wherry lines.org.uk*) goes east to Great Yarmouth and Lowestoft. Book in advance if you want to take a bike *0845 600 7245*.

National Express East Anglia for rail travel throughout the region *0870 333 4876*; *www.nationalexpresseastanglia.com*.

National Rail Enquiries, for information and booking *08457 484950*; *www.nationalrail.co.uk*.

Traveline for public transport information in south and east England *0871 200 2233*; *www.travelineeastanglia.org.uk*.

WALKING
Ramblers. The association campaigns for, and encourages, walkers *020 7339 8500*; *www.ramblers.org.uk*.

The Wherryman's Way, a long distance footpath *www.wherrymansway.net*.

Walking in Norfolk *www.walkinginnorfolk.co.uk*.

Walking in Suffolk *www.walkinginsuffolk.co.uk*.

WATER SKIING
British Water Ski, the national governing body for British water skiing *01932 570885*; *www.britishwaterski.org.uk*.

Easter Rivers Water Ski Club, for water skiing on the Broads *www.erwsc.co.uk*.

WEATHER FORECAST
For the Met Office weather forecast for Norfolk, Suffolk and Cambridgeshire telephone Weathercall on *09014 722058* or visit *www.metoffice.gov.uk*.

Weather forecasts and tide tables are available from the BBC *www.bbc.co.uk/weather/coast*.

WEIL'S DISEASE
Leptospirosis Information Centre, for information and advice *www.leptospirosis.org*.

WILDLIFE RESCUE
RSPCA *0300 123 0709*.

Boat trips run from Fairhaven Woodland & Water Garden, see Places to Visit, page 94.

Listed below is a selection of places to eat featured in the annual Broads Authority *Eating Out Guide 2010*. All have been visited by one of their inspectors as part of the Broads Quality Charter. This scheme showcases local food and excellence. The Ⓜ symbol indicates mooring nearby.

ACLE (page 53) **Bridge Inn** *Acle Bridge, Old Road, Acle, Norfolk NR13 3AS (01493 750288; www.maypolehotels.com).* Riverside pub and restaurant. Ⓜ

Hermitage Restaurant & Bar *64 Old Road, Acle, Norfolk NR13 3QP (01493 750310; www.thehermitageltd.co.uk).* Pub and restaurant. Ⓜ

BARNBY (page 66) **Swan Inn** *Swan Lane, Barnby, near Beccles, Suffolk NR34 7QF (01502 476646).* Lots of seafood, as well as meat and vegetarian dishes.

BECCLES (page 65) **Kings Head Hotel** *New Market, Beccles, Suffolk NR34 9HA (01502 712147; www.kingsheadhotel beccles.co.uk).* Hotel, bar and restaurant. Ⓜ

Swan House Restaurant *By St Michael's tower, Beccles, Suffolk NR34 9HH (01502 713474; www.swan-house.com).* Bar and *à la carte* menu of seasonal dishes. Advance booking recommended. Ⓜ

BRUNDALL (page 51) **The Lavender House** *39 The Street, Brundall, Norfolk NR13 5AA (01603 712215; www.thelavenderhouse.co.uk).* Restaurant and cookery school. Booking advised.

CLIPPESBY (page 45) **Susie's Coffee Shop** *Clippesby Hall, Clippesby, Great Yarmouth, Norfolk NR29 3BL (01493 367800; www.clipesby.com).* Meals served all day. Bread baked daily. *See also* Where to Hire, page 75.

COLTISHALL (page 42) **Andaman Orchid** *41 Church Street, Coltishall, Norfolk NR12 7DW (01603 736655;* *www.coltishall.org.uk).* Comfortable Thai restaurant. Ⓜ

Norfolk Mead Hotel *Coltishall, Norfolk NR12 7DN (01603 737531; www.norfolkmead.co.uk).* Once a Georgian merchant's house, now a hotel and restaurant. Ⓜ

FILBY (page 46) **Filby Bridge Restaurant** *Main Road, Filby, Great Yarmouth, Norfolk NR29 3AA (01493 368142; www.filbybridgerestaurant.com).* Morning coffee, lunches, evening meals and *à la carte* menu (booking required).

GELDESTON (page 64) **Wherry Inn** *The Street, Geldeston, Beccles, Suffolk NR34 0LB (01508 518371).* Real ales, bar and restaurant meals. Children welcome. Ⓜ

GREAT YARMOUTH (page 55) **White Swan** *1 North Quay, Great Yarmouth, Norfolk NR30 1PU (01493 842027).* Home cooked pub meals. Ⓜ

HICKLING (page 40) **Greyhound Inn** *The Green, Hickling, Norfolk NR12 0YA (01692 598306; www.greyhoundinn.com).* Real ale, bar and restaurant meals. Ⓜ

HORNING (page 43) **Bure River Cottage Restaurant** *27 Lower Street, Horning, Norfolk NR12 8AA (01692 631421).* Speciality fish and seafood restaurant. Ⓜ

The Gallery @ Horning *43 Lower Street, Horning, Norfolk NR12 8AA (01692 630088).* Well-stocked delicatessen. Bread baked on the premises. Ⓜ

HORSEY (page 41) **Nelson Head** *The Street, Horsey, Norfolk NR29 4AD (01493 393378; www.nelsonheadhorsey.co.uk).* Bar and restaurant. Real ale. Dogs welcome, except at meal times.

HORSTEAD (page 42) **Recruiting Sergeant** *Norwich Road, Horstead, Norwich, Norfolk NR12 7EE (01603 737077;*

www.recruitingsergeant.co.uk). Pub offering snacks and restaurant meals. Real ale.

HOVETON (page 42) **The Old Barn**
Wroxham Barns *Tunstead Road, Hoveton, Norfolk NR12 8QU (01603 783911; www.wroxhambarns.co.uk).*
Café and restaurant.

LODDON (page 57) **Rosy Lee's Tea Room**
37 Bridge Street, Loddon, Norwich NR14 6NA (01508 520204). Daily specials and cakes from the local Women's Institute.

LUDHAM (page 44) **Alfresco Tea Rooms**
Norwich Road, Ludham, Norfolk NR29 5QA (01692 678 384; www.alfrescotearooms.co.uk). Traditional tearoom in thatched cottage.

Kings Arms *High Street, Ludham, Norfolk NR29 5QQ (01692 678386; www.kingsarmsludham.co.uk).* Bar and restaurant. Children's play area.

OULTON BROAD (page 66) **Red Herring**
152 Bridge Road, Oulton Broad, Suffolk NR33 9JT (01502 566499; www.redherringrestaurant.co.uk). Restaurant, tapas and wine bar.

The Waveney *134 Bridge Road, Oulton Broad, Suffolk NR33 9JT (01502 573940).* Family pub serving real ale and meals. Children welcome.

POTTER HEIGHAM (page 45) **Riverside Tea Rooms** *Bridge Road, Potter Heigham, Great Yarmouth, Norfolk NR29 5JD (01692 671719).* By the river.

RANWORTH (page 43) **Granary Stores & Tea Shop** *Ranworth Staithe, Ranworth, Norfolk NR13 6AY (01603 270432).* Made-to-order sandwiches and ploughman's, together with homebaking.

REEDHAM (page 59) **Reedham Ferry Inn**
Reedham Ferry, Norfolk NR13 3HA (01493 700429; www.archerstouring park.co.uk). Bar and restaurant meals. Real ale. Children welcome.

ROCKLAND ST MARY (page 57) **New Inn**
12 New Inn Hill, Rockland St Mary, Norfolk NR14 7HP (01508 538403). Pub and restaurant.

SOMERLEYTON (page 66) **Dukes Head**
Slugs Lane, Somerleyton, Suffolk NR32 5QR (01502 730281; www.somerleyton.co.uk). Pub and restaurant.

SOUTH WALSHAM (page 44)
Fairhaven Woodland & Water Garden
School Road, South Walsham, Norfolk NR13 6DZ (01603 270449/270683; www.fairhavengarden.co.uk). Specialising in food for vegetarians, coeliacs and diabetics, but welcoming to all. *See also* Places to Visit, page 94.

Kings Arms Pub and Chinese & Thai Restaurant *1 Panxworth Road, South Walsham, Norfolk NR13 6DY (01603 270039; www.broadlandchinese.co.uk).* Eat-in or takeaway. Real ale and Chinese beer.

Ship Inn *18 The Street, South Walsham, Norfolk NR13 6DQ (01603 270049; www.theshipsouthwalsham.co.uk).* Pub and restaurant. Real ale. Dogs welcome.

STOKESBY (page 53) **Riverside Tea Room and Stores** *The Green, Stokesby, Norfolk NR29 3EX (01493 750470; www.stokesby.org.uk).* General store, which also serves meals all day.

SURLINGHAM (page 51) **The Ferry House**
Ferry Road, Surlingham, Norfolk NR14 7AR (01508 538659; www.surlinghamferryhouse. co.uk). Traditional pub fare.

THURNE (page 44) **The Lion Inn** *The Street, Thurne, Norfolk NR29 3AP (01692 670796; www.lion-inn-thurne.co.uk).* Bar and restaurant meals. Real ale. Also showers and general store.

WOODBASTWICK (page 43) **Fur and Feather Inn** *Slad Lane, Woodbastwick, Norwich, Norfolk NR13 6HQ (01603 720003; www.thefurandfeatherinn.co.uk).* Pub and restaurant. Real ale.

Average clearance at high water is given but always check bridge gauge boards. Think ahead when approaching all bridges. Lower the canopy and/or windscreen. Get everyone off the deck. Ensure that all hands and heads are inboard in plenty of time before bridge. *See also* Navigation Notes, page 14.

SPEED LIMIT

Speed limits range from 3 to 6 mph – please comply with them. Look out for the warning signs. *See also* Boating Need to Know, page 13.

CAUTION

Water ski area. Keep a steady course to the right hand side of the channel. *See also* Boating Need to Know, page 13.

Overhead cables.

Yachts must lower their masts at all bridges except Reedham, Somerleyton and Trowse swing bridges, the lifting bridges on Breydon Water, the Novi Sad swing pedestrian bridge in Norwich and the lifting bridge at Carrow Road, Norwich.

There are set times at which Trowse rail bridge opens *(see www.broads-authority.gov.uk)*. The Broads Authority website also has a list of bridge clearance measurements. These are given for Average High Water during the summer. Note that there will be greater clearance at Low Water, especially at Great Yarmouth and in the southern rivers. As well as the state of the tide, river levels can be affected by rainfall and wind conditions. Always exercise caution when approaching any bridge and carefully note the bridge gauge board. *See also* Navigation Notes, page 44.

Rivers Bure, Ant and Thurne — hours

From \ To	Ant Mouth	Barton Broad	Coltishall	Great Yarmouth	Hickling Staithe	Horning	Potter Heigham	Stalham	Stracey Arms Mill	Thurne Mouth	Wroxham
Acle	1	2¼	4¾	2¼	2½	2	1¼	3	1	½	3¼
Ant Mouth		1¼	3¾	3¼	2½	1	1¼	2	2	½	2¼
Barton Broad			5	4¾	3¾	2¼	2½	¾	3¼	1¾	3½
Coltishall				7¼	6¼	2¾	5	5¾	5¾	4¼	1½
Great Yarmouth					4¾	4½	3¾	5½	1½	3	5½
Hickling Staithe						3½	1¼	4½	3¼	2	4½
Horning							2¼	3	3	1½	1¼
Potter Heigham								3¼	2¼	¾	3½
Stalham									4	2½	4¼
Stracey Arms Mill										1½	4
Thurne Mouth											2¾

Rivers Yare, Chet and Waveney — hours

From \ To	Beccles	Berney Arms Mill	Brundall	Burgh Castle	Cantley	Geldeston	Great Yarmouth	Loddon	Norwich Yacht Station	Oulton Broad Yacht Station	Oulton Dyke	Reedham	St Olaves
Berney Arms Mill	4												
Brundall	5½	3											
Burgh Castle	3¾	¼	3¼										
Cantley	4¼	1¾	1¼	2									
Geldeston	1	5	6½	4¾	5¼								
Great Yarmouth	4¾	¾	3¾	1	2¾	5¾							
Loddon	4¾	2¼	2¾	2½	1½	5¾	3						
Norwich Yacht Station	7½	5	2	5¼	3¼	8½	5¾	4¾					
Oulton Broad Yacht Station	2¼	2¾	4¼	2½	3	3¼	3½	3½	6¼				
Oulton Dyke	1¾	2¼	3¾	2	2½	2¾	3	3	5¾	½			
Reedham	3¼	1	2	1¼	1	4¼	1¾	1¼	4	2¼	1¾		
St Olaves	2¾	1¼	2¾	1	1¾	3¾	2	2	4¾	1½	1	¾	
Thorpe Green	6¾	4½	1½	4¾	2½	7¾	5¼	4¼	½	5¾	5¼	3½	4¼

Waterways Signs and Journey Times

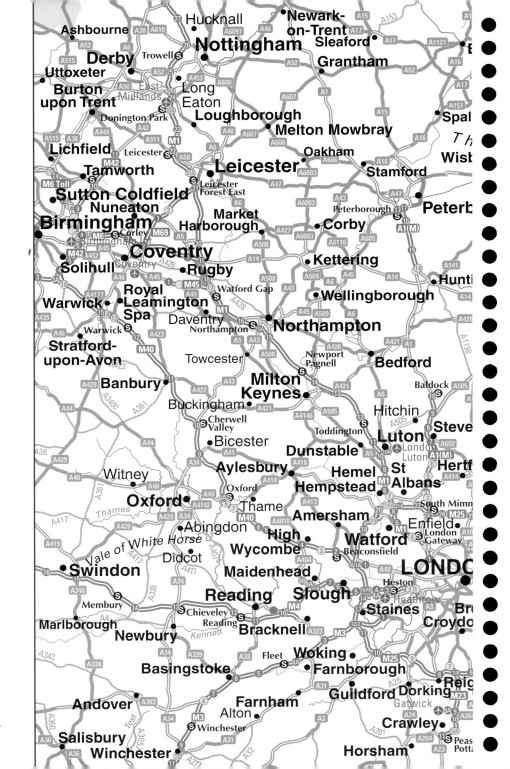

The Wash

Boston

Blakeney Point

Cromer

The

Wash

Hunstanton

ding

King's Lynn

Dereham

Norwich International

Great Yarmouth

e Fens

Swaffham

Norwich

ech

Downham Market

The Broads

Yare

orough

Thetford Forest

Lowestoft

Beccles

Ely

Thetford

Diss

Mildenhall

Park

Waveney

ngdon

Bury St Edmunds

Newmarket

Stowmarket

Cambridge

Haverhill

Ipswich

Woodbridge

Sudbury

Saffron Walden

Harwich

Felixstowe

nage

Stansted

Braintree

Colchester

Birchanger Green

Clacton-on-Sea

ord

Harlow

Witham

Chelmsford

Maldon

Cheshunt

Crouch

Brentwood

Romford

Basildon

London Southend

Ilford

Southend-on-Sea

Thurrock

Canvey Island

London City

River Thames

Dartford

Tilbury

Gravesend

Sheerness

Isle of Sheppey

Herne Bay

Margate

North Foreland

omley

n

Chatham

Medway

Sittingbourne

Kent International

Ramsgate

Clacket Lane

Maidstone

Canterbury

Sevenoaks

Maidstone

Deal

ate

East Grinstead

Tonbridge

Ashford

Royal Tunbridge Wells

Stop 24

Dover

e nge

The Weald

Crowborough

Folkestone

Strait of Dover

33

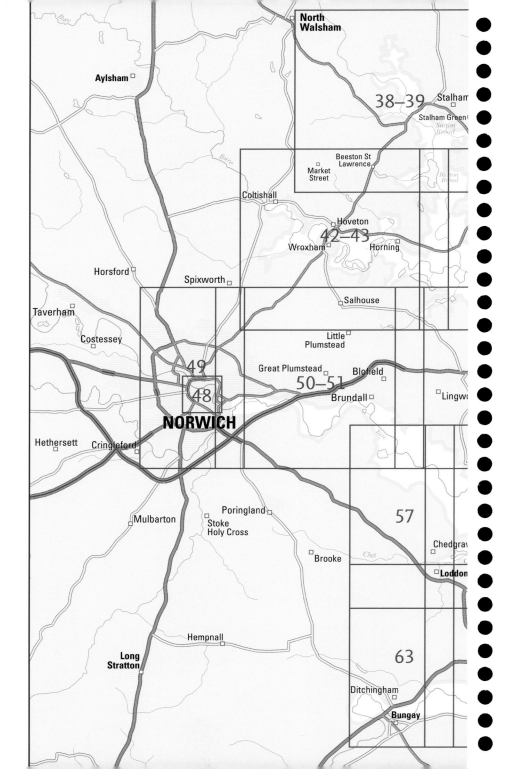

North Walsham

Aylsham

38–39

Stalham

Stalham Green

Beeston St Lawrence

Market Street

Coltishall

Hoveton

42–43

Wroxham

Horning

Horsford

Spixworth

Salhouse

Taverham

Little Plumstead

Costessey

Great Plumstead

Blofield

49

50–51

Brundall

Lingwood

48

NORWICH

Hethersett

Cringleford

Mulbarton

Poringland

Stoke Holy Cross

57

Chedgrave

Brooke

Loddon

Hempnall

63

Long Stratton

Ditchingham

Bungay

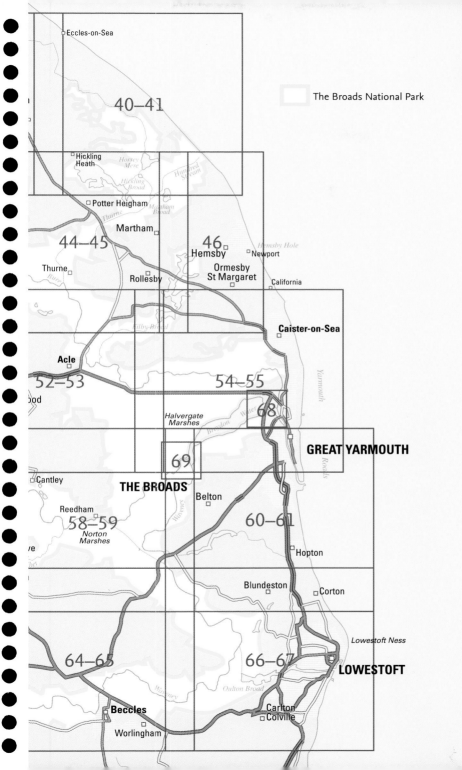

The Broads National Park

40–41

Eccles-on-Sea

Hickling
Heath

*Horsey
Mere*

*Hundred
Stream*

*Hickling
Broad*

Potter Heigham

Thurne

*Martham
Broad*

Martham

44–45

Hemsby

46

Hemsby Hole

Newport

Thurne

Bure

Rollesby

Ormesby
St Margaret

California

Filby Broad

Caister-on-Sea

Acle

52–53

ood

54–55

Yarmouth

68

Halvergate
Marshes

Breydon Water

GREAT YARMOUTH

69

Cantley

THE BROADS

Roads

Belton

Reedham

58–59

Norton
Marshes

Waveney

60–61

Hopton

ve

Blundeston

Corton

Lowestoft Ness

64–65

66–67

Waveney

Oulton Broad

LOWESTOFT

Beccles

Worlingham

Carlton
Colville

KEY TO SYMBOLS

Mutford Lock ⚓ Lock

M Broads Authority mooring, free, max. 24 hours

M Other mooring (selected)

Boatyard B

Hire centre H

Diesel D

Water point 🚰

Recycling ♺

Boat trips 🚤

Public slipway

Overhead cables

P Petrol

E Electric boat recharging

Sewage or 'Elsan' disposal point

Refuse disposal point

Pump out

Fishing platform

Strongly tidal navigation
Marginally tidal navigation

Shipping channel – no hire craft

Water ski area – keep to the right side of channel

Ludham Bridge Bridge, with name and clearance;
2.60 m (8′ 6″) metres (feet)

Waymarked long-distance footpaths

Other paths – only indicated where close to broads/dykes and rivers

You will see many places using the term **staithe** on the map. The word comes from the Norse language and means a landing stage or wharf.

Moveable bridge (Lower canopies, windscreens etc. Take extra care.)

Arch bridge

Arch bridge (Lower canopies, windscreens etc. Take extra care.)
Clearance is given at the centre of arch bridges.

Navigation posts

45 Continuation page number

i Broads Information Centre

i Tourist Information Centre

Historic building

Mill or wind pump

Museum

Nature reserve

★ Other place of interest

Broads walk

Boardwalk (suitable for wheelchairs and pushchairs)

Scale 1 : 50 000

0 km   0.5   1   2   3   4

0 miles   0.5   1   2

Berney Arms Mill.

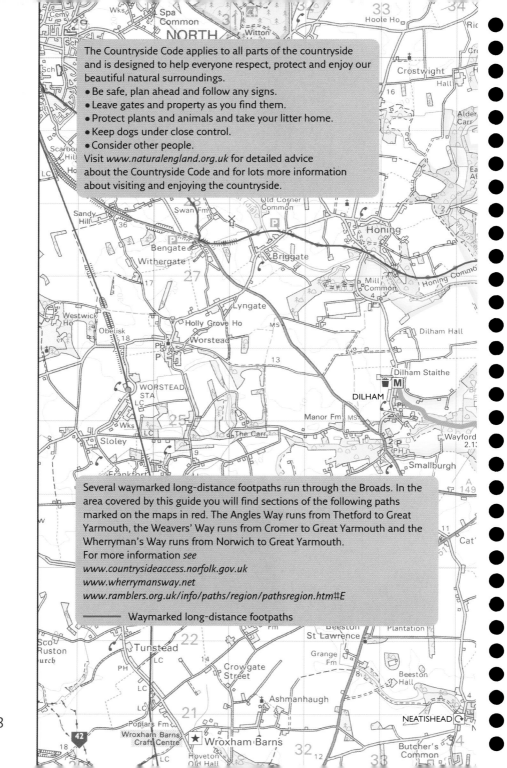

The Countryside Code applies to all parts of the countryside and is designed to help everyone respect, protect and enjoy our beautiful natural surroundings.
• Be safe, plan ahead and follow any signs.
• Leave gates and property as you find them.
• Protect plants and animals and take your litter home.
• Keep dogs under close control.
• Consider other people.
Visit *www.naturalengland.org.uk* for detailed advice about the Countryside Code and for lots more information about visiting and enjoying the countryside.

Several waymarked long-distance footpaths run through the Broads. In the area covered by this guide you will find sections of the following paths marked on the maps in red. The Angles Way runs from Thetford to Great Yarmouth, the Weavers' Way runs from Cromer to Great Yarmouth and the Wherryman's Way runs from Norwich to Great Yarmouth.
For more information *see*
www.countrysideaccess.norfolk.gov.uk
www.wherrymansway.net
www.ramblers.org.uk/info/paths/region/pathsregion.htm#E

———————— Waymarked long-distance footpaths

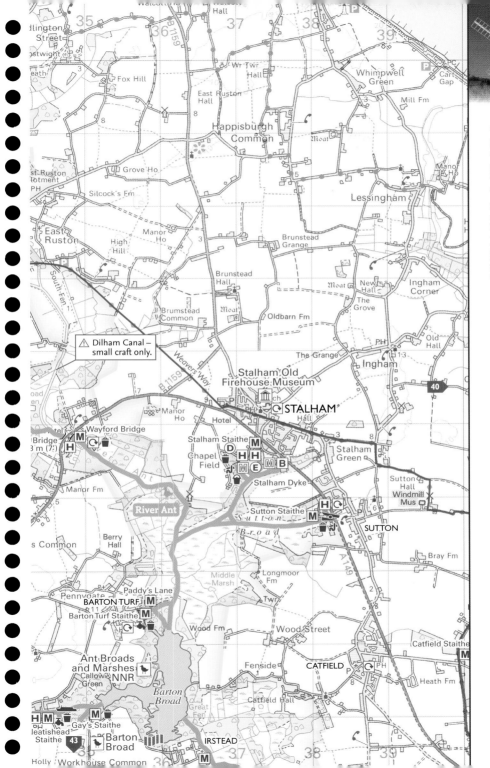

⚠ Dilham Canal –
small craft only.

Watcotting
Hall
[P]
[PC]
Cart
Gap

35 36 37 38 39

dlington
Street
ostwight
eath

Fox Hill

Wr Twr
Hall

Whimpwell
Green

Mill Fm

B1159

East Ruston
Hall

Happisburgh
Common

Moat

Manor
Ho

Grove Ho

st Ruston
llotment
PH

Silcock's Fm

Lessingham

East
Ruston

High
Hill

Manor
Ho

Brunstead
Grange

[P]

South Fen

Brunstead
Hall

Moat

New
Hall

Ingham
Corner

Brumstead
Common

Moat

Oldbarn Fm

The
Grove

Old
Hall

Weavers Way

The Grange

PH

Ingham

13

B1159

Stalham Old
Firehouse Museum

[40]

oad
en

Manor
Ho

Hotel

[P]

ch

○ STALHAM

Stalham
Hall

Wayford Bridge

Field

[H] [M] ○ 🗑

Stalham Staithe

Stalham
Green

Bridge
3 m (7)

Chapel
Field

[D] [M] [H] [H]
[H] [M] [B]
[M] [E]

River Ant

Manor Fm

Stalham Dyke

Sutton
Hall

Windmill
Mus

Sutton Staithe

Sutton
Broad

[H] ○
[M]

SUTTON

Berry
Hall

s Common

River Ant

A149

Bray Fm

Middle
Marsh

Longmoor
Fm

Pennygate

Paddy's Lane

BARTON TURF [M]

Twr

Barton Turf Staithe [M]

○ 🗑

Wood Fm

Wood Street

Catfield Staithe

Ant Broads
and Marshes
NNR

Callow
Green

Fenside

CATFIELD ○ PH

Heath Fm

[M]

[H] [M] 🗑 [M] 🗑

Gay's Staithe

leatishead
Staithe [43]

Barton
Broad

Barton
Broad

Great
Fen

Catfield Hall

IRSTEAD

[M]

Holly Workhouse Common

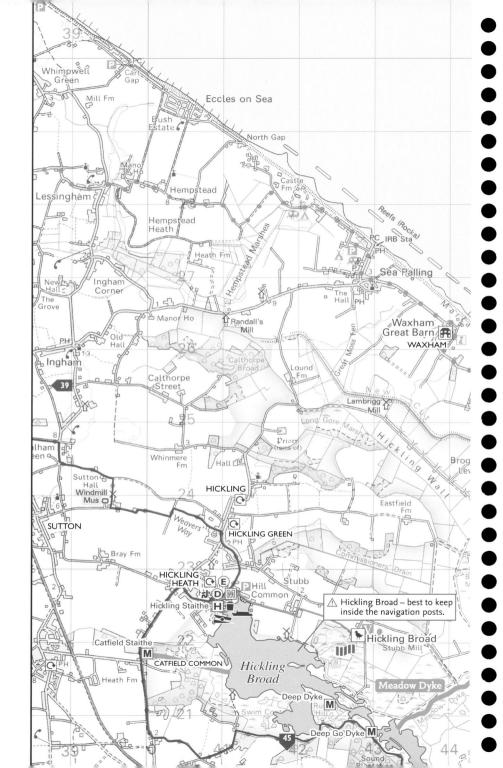

Whimpwell Green

Mill Fm

Eccles on Sea

Bush Estate

North Gap

Manor Ho

Castle Fm

Lessingham

Hempstead

Hempstead Heath

Reefs (Rocks)

Heath Fm

PC   IRB Sta

PH

Sea Palling

New Hall

Ingham Corner

The Grove

Manor Ho

Randall's Mill

The Hall   PH

Waxham Great Barn

WAXHAM

PH

Old Hall

Ingham

39

Calthorpe Street

Calthorpe Broad

Lound Fm

Lambrigg Mill

Priory (rems of)

Long Gore Marsh

Hickling Wall

Whinmere Fm

Hall

Sutton Hall Windmill Mus

HICKLING

HICKLING GREEN

PH

Eastfield Fm

SUTTON

Weavers' Way

Bray Fm

Commissioners' Drain

HICKLING HEATH

E

P Hill Common

Stubb

Hickling Staithe

D **M**

H

⚠ Hickling Broad – best to keep inside the navigation posts.

Catfield Staithe

M

CATFIELD COMMON

Hickling Broad

Heath Fm

Hickling Broad

Stubb Mill

Meadow Dyke

Deep Dyke

M

Swim Coot

45

Deep Go'Dyke

M

Sound

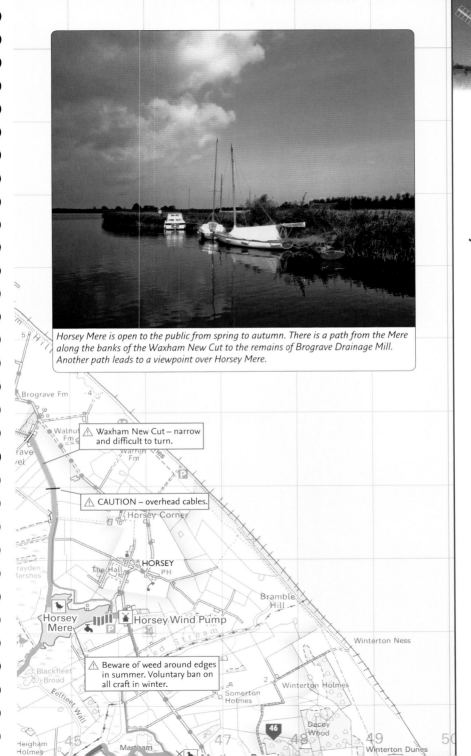

Horsey Mere is open to the public from spring to autumn. There is a path from the Mere along the banks of the Waxham New Cut to the remains of Brograve Drainage Mill. Another path leads to a viewpoint over Horsey Mere.

Brograve Fm

Walnut Fm

rave vel

⚠ Waxham New Cut – narrow and difficult to turn.

Warren Fm

P

⚠ CAUTION – overhead cables.

Horsey Corner

rayden Marshes

The Hall

HORSEY
PH

Bramble Hill

Horsey Mere

Horsey Wind Pump

PC

P

Winterton Ness

Blackfleet Broad

⚠ Beware of weed around edges in summer. Voluntary ban on all craft in winter.

Somerton Holmes

Winterton Holmes

Eelfleet Wall

Decoy Wood

46

45

Marham

47

48

49

50

Heigham Holmes

Winterton Dunes

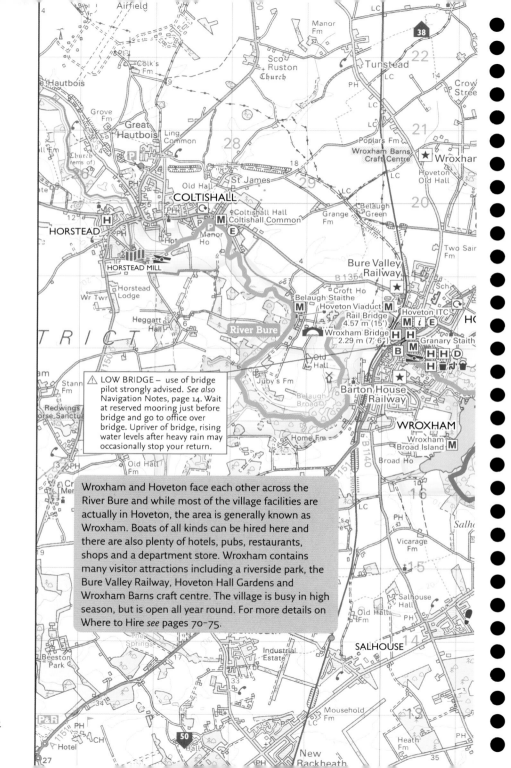

⚠ LOW BRIDGE – use of bridge pilot strongly advised. *See also Navigation Notes, page 14.* Wait at reserved mooring just before bridge and go to office over bridge. Upriver of bridge, rising water levels after heavy rain may occasionally stop your return.

Wroxham and Hoveton face each other across the River Bure and while most of the village facilities are actually in Hoveton, the area is generally known as Wroxham. Boats of all kinds can be hired here and there are also plenty of hotels, pubs, restaurants, shops and a department store. Wroxham contains many visitor attractions including a riverside park, the Bure Valley Railway, Hoveton Hall Gardens and Wroxham Barns craft centre. The village is busy in high season, but is open all year round. For more details on Where to Hire *see pages 70-75.*

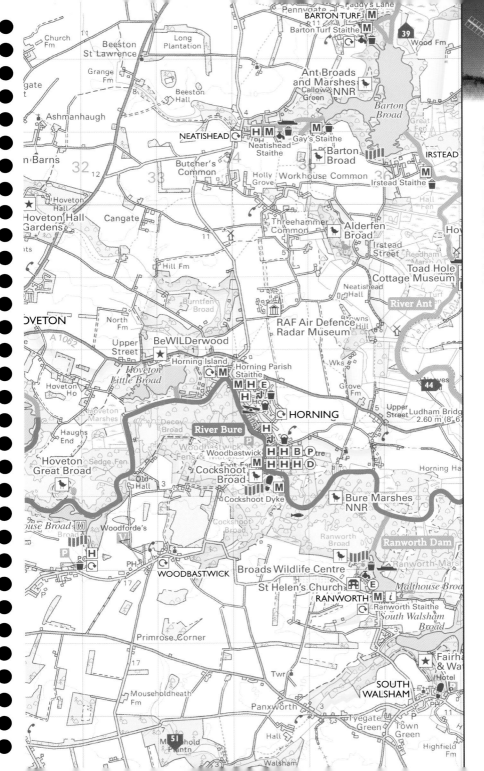

River Ant

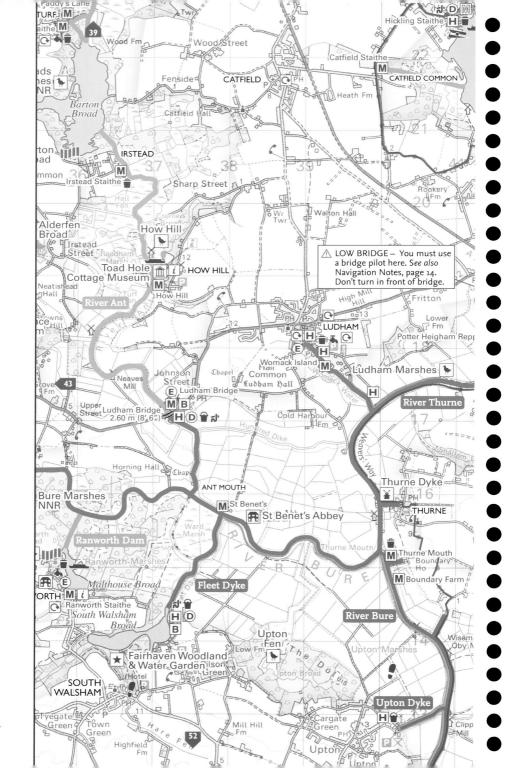

⚠ LOW BRIDGE – You must use a bridge pilot here. *See also* Navigation Notes, page 14. Don't turn in front of bridge.

⚠ Hickling Broad – best to keep inside the navigation posts.

40

Hickling Broad
Stubb Mill

Horsey Mere

PC

Horsey Wind Pump

P

Hickling Broad

Meadow Dyke

Blackfleet Broad

⚠ Beware of weed around edges in summer. Voluntary ban on all craft in winter.

Deep Dyke M

Rush Hill

Swim Co

Deep Go'Dyke M

42

Sound Plantation

44 Heigham Holmes

45 Martham Broad

Eelfleet Wall

Martham

West Somerton M

Martham

WEST SOMER

Hall Fm

3

POTTER HEIGHAM

High's Mill

Martham Ferry

B D Martham
H   Ferry
   P

Moregrove

Damgate
Wr Twr

19

i H

Potter Heigham Bridge Green

New Bridge 2.36 m (7' 9")
Old Bridge 2.03 m (6' 8")
(rems of)

Mustard Hyrn

Thunder Hill 16

C B H M
ꝛ P M M E
s Bank Potter Heigham Martham Bank
Repps H
Le

Cess

MARTHAM

PH

BASTWICK

5

Hall Fms 46

REPPS C

5

Sailing on the River Thurne.

MS

ROLLESBY BRIDGE

Ormesby Bro

Dei

Glebe Fm

ate

PC

Rollesby Broad

H

Manor Fm

Clippesby Ho

Clippesby

Fleggburgh
(Burgh St Margaret)

Lily Broad

Church
(rems of)

P

an's ill

H CLIPPESBY HALL

PH

Leisure Centre

P

Oby

South House Fm

11

B1152

Hall

A1064

Billockby

4

Newgate Corner

The Nab

MS

Filby Broad

esby

1

53

Burgh Common

THRIGBY

Croft Fm

Thrigby H
Wildlife G

45

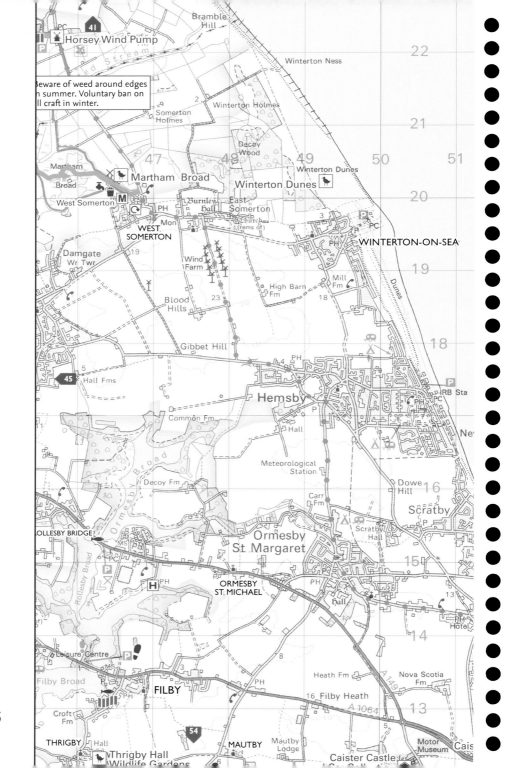

Bramble Hill

PC
41
Horsey Wind Pump

Beware of weed around edges
in summer. Voluntary ban on
all craft in winter.

Winterton Ness

Winterton Holmes

Somerton Holmes

2

22

Decoy Wood

47   48   49   Winterton Dunes   50   51

Martham Broad

Martham Broad   Martham Broad   Winterton Dunes

21

West Somerton   M

WEST SOMERTON   PH   Burnley Hall   East Somerton   3   PC
Mon   Church (rems of)   P
PH   WINTERTON-ON-SEA

20

Damgate   Wr Twr
19   Wind Farm   Mill Fm   Dunes

19

Blood Hills   High Barn Fm   18

23

Gibbet Hill   PH   4   18

45   5   Hall Fms   Hemsby   P   IRB Sta   PC
PH

Common Fm   Hall

Meteorological Station

Ne

Decoy Fm   Carr Fm   Dowe Hill   16   Scratby
Scratby Hall

OLLESBY BRIDGE   MS   Ormesby St Margaret   15
PC   P

H   PH   ORMESBY ST. MICHAEL   Hall   PH   13
PH   Hotel

14

Leisure Centre   P   8   Heath Fm   Nova Scotia Fm
MS   Filby Broad   PH   16 Filby Heath   A 1064   13
FILBY   3   A 149
Croft Fm
THRIGBY   54   MAUTBY   Mautby Lodge   Motor Museum   Cais
Thrigby Hall   Mautby   Caister Castle
Wildlife Gardens

Public moorings extend down either side of the dyke at Thurne and it is a good place to moor up. At the head of the dyke is Thurne Dyke Mill, owned by the Norfolk Windmills Trust (www.norfolkwindmills.co.uk). The mill was built in 1820, but the sails and cap were blown off in 1919 and it needed repair. At some stage, the mill was extended in height and this gives it the distinctive shape, as the new section was made round to allow the cap to be re-used. See Places to Visit, page 88.

Norwich Yacht Station, Riverside Road, Norwich (01603 612980).

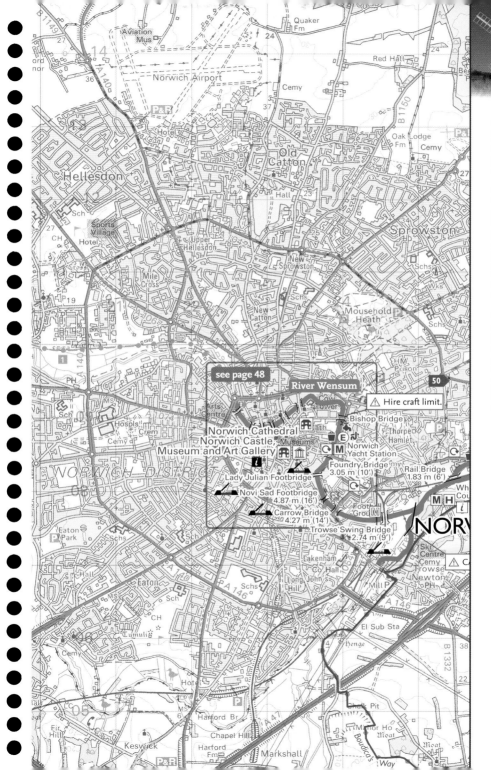

see page 48

River Wensum

⚠ Hire craft limit.

Bishop Bridge

Norwich Cathedral
Norwich Castle,
Museum and Art Gallery

Museums

Norwich
Yacht Station

Lady Julian Footbridge

Foundry Bridge
3.05 m (10')

Rail Bridge
1.83 m (6')

Novi Sad Footbridge
4.87 m (16')

Carrow Bridge
4.27 m (14')

Trowse Swing Bridge
2.74 m (9')

NOR

50

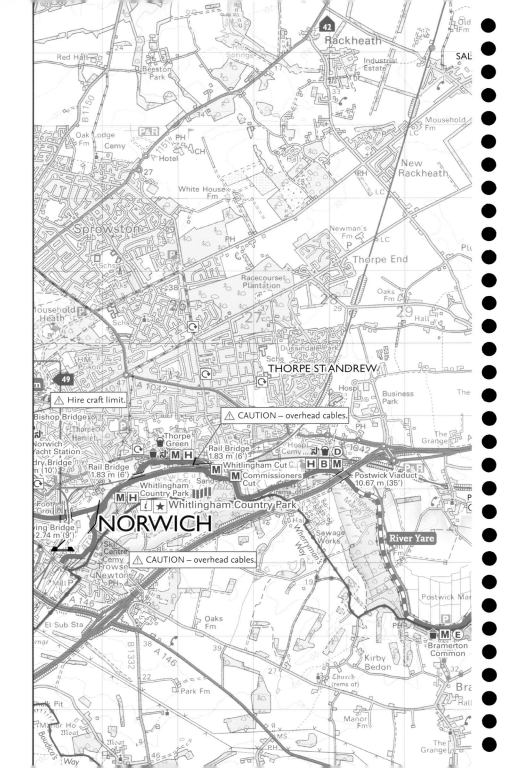

Rackheath

Industrial Estate

SAL

Old Fm

42

Red Hall

Beeston Park

The Springs

New Rackheath

Mousehold Fm

LC

Oak Lodge Fm

P&R

Cemy

PH

Hotel

CH

White House Fm

Hall

PH

LC

Sprowston

Newman's Fm

Thorpe End

Racecourse Plantation

P

LC

Schs

Wks

Oaks Fm

Household Heath

Schs

Dussindale Park

THORPE ST ANDREW

HM Prison

Hospl

Business Park

The

49

Hire craft limit.

Bishop Bridge

Thorpe Hamlet

Thorpe Green

CAUTION – overhead cables.

Hospl Cemy

PH

The Grange

Norwich Yacht Station

M H

Rail Bridge 1.83 m (6')

P&R

dry Bridge m (10')

Rail Bridge 1.83 m (6')

M

Whitlingham Cut

Commissioners Cut

H B M

Postwick Viaduct 10.67 m (35')

Whitlingham Country Park

M

Sand

Crems off

P&R

M H

i ★ Whitlingham Country Park

River Yare

NORWICH

Whitlingham Marsh

Foot Grou

M

Wherryman's Way

Sewage Works

Hall Fm

ing Bridge 2.74 m (9')

Ski Centre

CAUTION – overhead cables.

Postwick M

Cemy

Trowse Newton

PH

P

Mill P

A 146

Oaks Fm

M E

Bramerton Common

El Sub Sta

B 1332

A 146

Kirby Bedon

Bra

Hall

50

Chalk Pit

Manor Ho Moat

Park Fm

Church (rems of)

Manor Fm

The Grange

Moat

MS

Boudica's Way

46

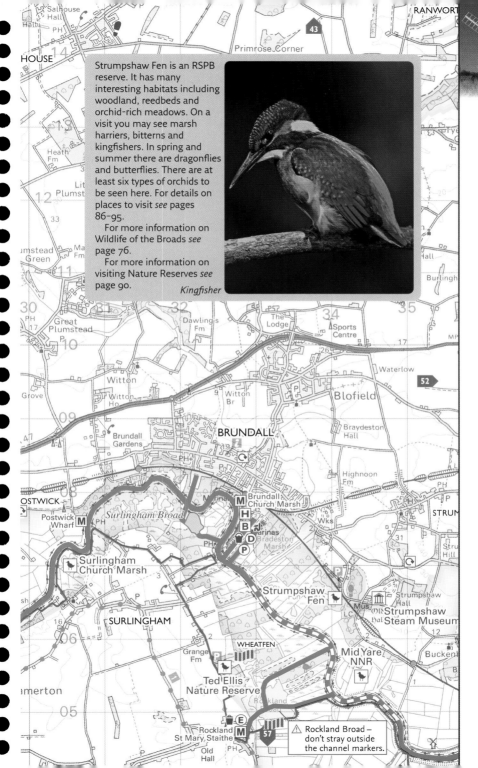

Strumpshaw Fen is an RSPB reserve. It has many interesting habitats including woodland, reedbeds and orchid-rich meadows. On a visit you may see marsh harriers, bitterns and kingfishers. In spring and summer there are dragonflies and butterflies. There are at least six types of orchids to be seen here. For details on places to visit *see* pages 86–95.

For more information on Wildlife of the Broads *see* page 76.

For more information on visiting Nature Reserves *see* page 90.

Kingfisher

⚠ Rockland Broad – don't stray outside the channel markers.

Boat hire is popular in the Broads as there are no locks to manage. The River Bure has many hire locations, either for a day trip or for a longer stay. For more details on Where to Hire see pages 70–75.

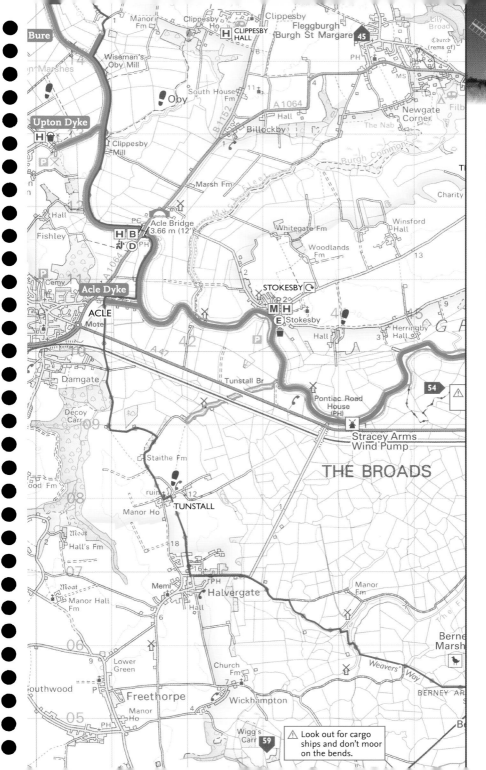

⚠ Look out for cargo ships and don't moor on the bends.

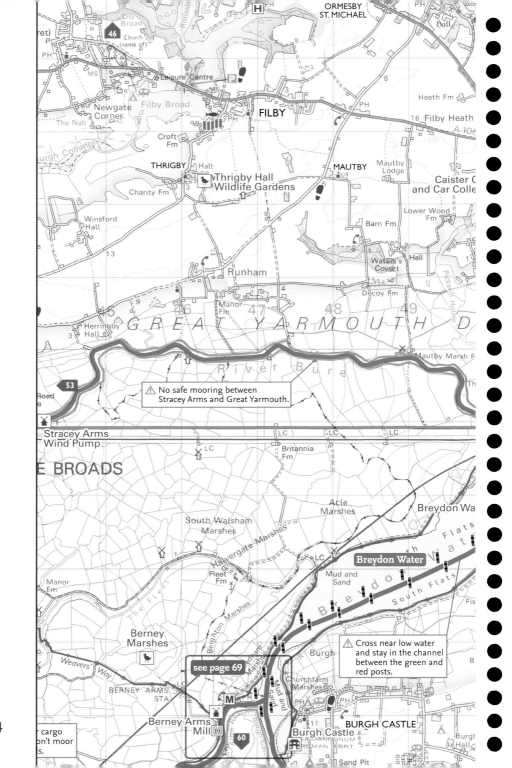

ORMESBY ST. MICHAEL

Hall

PH

46

Church (rems of)

PH

Lily Broad

Leisure Centre

P

MS

Newgate Corner

The Nab

Filby Broad

FILBY

Heath Fm

PH

16 Filby Heath

A 106

Croft Fm

THRIGBY

Hall

Thrigby Hall Wildlife Gardens

MAUTBY

Mautby Lodge

Caister
and Car Coll

Charity Fm

Winsford Hall

13

Barn Fm

Lower Wood Fm

Waters's Covert

Hall

Runham

Decoy Fm

Manor Fm

Pickell Ho

45

46

47

48

49

G R E A T   Y A R M O U T H   D

Herringby Hall

Mautby Marsh F

River Bure

Th

53

Road

⚠ No safe mooring between
Stracey Arms and Great Yarmouth.

Stracey Arms
Wind Pump

E BROADS

LC

LC

LC

LC

Britannia Fm

Acle Marshes

Breydon Wa

South Walsham Marshes

Halvergate Marshes

LC

Breydon Water

Fleet Fm

Mud and Sand

Breydon Wate

South Flats

Manor Fm

The Fleet

Beighton Marshes

Berney Marshes

Burgh

⚠ Cross near low water
and stay in the channel
between the green and
red posts.

Weavers' Way

see page 69

BERNEY ARMS STA.

M

Berney Arms
Mill M

60

Churchfarm Marshes

PH

PH

BURGH CASTLE

54

cargo
on't moor
s.

Burgh Castle
GARIANNONUM
ROMAN FORT

Sand Pit

Burgh
Hall

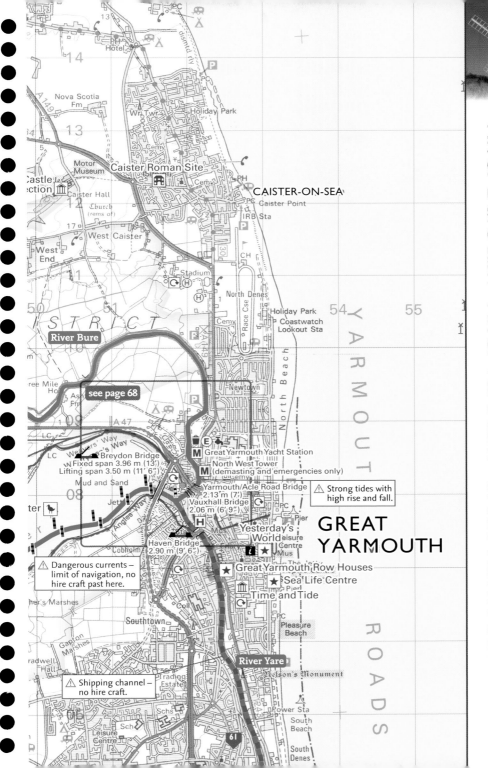

Nova Scotia Fm

Wr Twr
Holiday Park

Motor Museum
Caister Roman Site

Castle ection
Caister Hall
Church (rems of)

CAISTER-ON-SEA
Caister Point
IRB Sta

West Caister

West End

Stadium

North Denes

STRICT

River Bure

Holiday Park
Coastwatch Lookout Sta

Cemy

see page 68

North Beach

Newtown

Ashy Frm

Three Mile Ho

LC
Weaver's Way

LC
Breydon Bridge
Fixed span 3.96 m (13')
Lifting span 3.50 m (11'6")

Mud and Sand

Jetty

Angles Way

North West Tower
(demasting and emergencies only)

Great Yarmouth Yacht Station

Yarmouth/Acle Road Bridge
2.13 m (7')
Vauxhall Bridge
2.06 m (6'9")

⚠ Strong tides with high rise and fall.

Pier

Yesterday's World

Haven Bridge
2.90 m (9'6")

Cobholm

Leisure Centre
Mus

★ Great Yarmouth Row Houses
★ Sea Life Centre
Time and Tide

⚠ Dangerous currents — limit of navigation, no hire craft past here.

her's Marshes

Southtown

Pleasure Beach

Coll

Gapton Marshes

adwell Hall

Trading Estate

River Yare

Nelson's Monument

⚠ Shipping channel — no hire craft.

Schs

Power Sta

South Beach

Leisure Centre

61

Schs

South Denes

YARMOUTH ROADS

GREAT YARMOUTH

Reedham Chain Ferry is an important crossing point on the River Yare for cars and pedestrians. See also Navigation Notes, page 17.

Reed and sedge has been cut and harvested in the Broads for centuries – the bundles of reed were transported from the reed beds by boat, using the network of dykes and rivers, which gave access to the nearby settlements. The reed was used to thatch buildings of all types, including churches and barns. Other vegetation was cut as feed and bedding for animals. The cutting process helped keep the traditional Broads landscape open by preventing the fens becoming overgrown by scrub and woodland, and provided a natural habitat for wildlife and plants. The commercial reed-cutting industry experienced a steady decline and had almost died out when, with assistance from the Broads Authority, the Broads Reed and Sedge Cutters Association *(www.reedcutters.norfolkbroads.com)* was formed in 2002.

This European award-winning project enabled both the Broads Authority and the association to access grants for training and cutting equipment, and has resulted in new reed cutters taking up the trade. It has also provided other work such as coppicing and scrub clearance, which helps provide the cutters with a stable income throughout the year. Although modern mowing equipment has been developed, the trade is still harsh work and labour intensive: reed is cut during the winter months, once frosts have removed the leaves from the reed stems; and hand tools are still used in vulnerable areas and during high tides. Sedge, more flexible than reed, is cut in the summer. Reed beds are now being restored and reed is being cut commercially on some sites for the first time in many years.

A trainee reed cutter near Sutton, Norfolk.

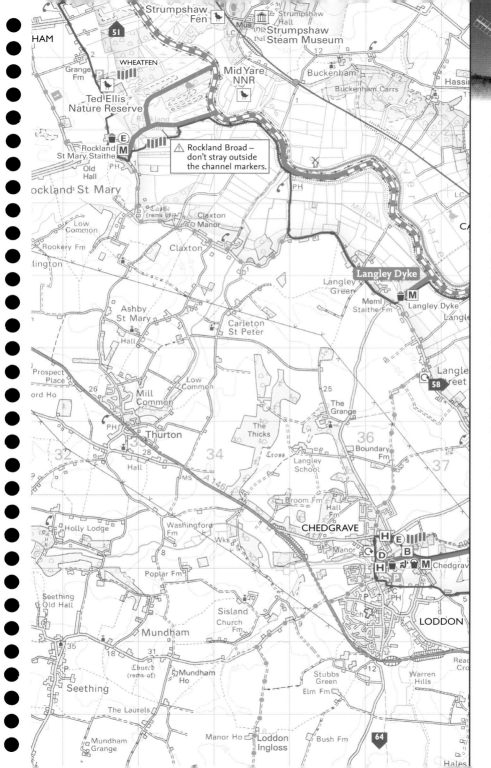

HAM

51

Strumpshaw Fen

Mus

Old Strumpshaw Hall

Strumpshaw Steam Museum

12

Grange Fm

WHEATFEN

Ted Ellis Nature Reserve

Mid Yare NNR

Buckenham

Buckenham Carrs

Hassi

2

Rockland

1

E

M

Rockland St Mary Staithe

⚠ Rockland Broad – don't stray outside the channel markers.

Old Hall

PH

River Yare

Mill Dike

LC

CA

ockland St Mary

PH

Castle (rems of)

Claxton Manor

Claxton

Langley Dyke

M

Low Common

Claxton

Langley Green

Meml Staithe Fm

Langley Dyke

Langl

Rookery Fm

lington

Ashby St Mary

Carleton St Peter

Hall

Langl Street

58

Prospect Place

26

Low Common

25

ord Ho

Mill Common

The Grange

Thurton

The Thicks

36

Boundary Fm

37

32

35

28

34

Cross

Langley School

Hall

MS

A146

Holly Lodge

Washingford Fm

Broom Fm

CHEDGRAVE

Hall Fm

H E E

Poplar Fm

Wks

Manor

D

B

H

M

Chedgrav

P

Seething Old Hall

8

PC

P

PH

5

Sisland Church Fm

Sch

LODDON

Mundham

35

18

31

Church (rems of)

Mundham Ho

Seething

Stubbs Green

Elm Fm

Warren Hills

Read Cr

12

The Laurels

Mundham Grange

Manor Ho

Loddon Ingloss

Bush Fm

64

Hale

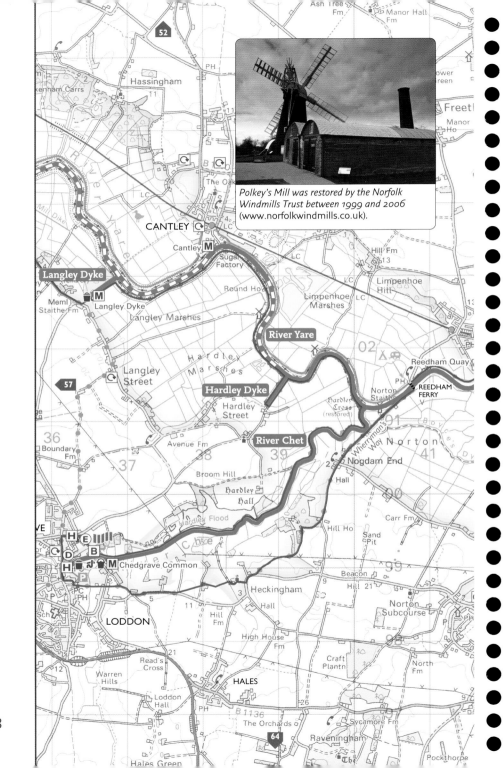

Polkey's Mill was restored by the Norfolk Windmills Trust between 1999 and 2006 (www.norfolkwindmills.co.uk).

52

Hassingham

kenham Carrs

11

PH

The Oak

CANTLEY

Cantley M

Sugar Factory

Langley Dyke

Meml
Staithe Fm

M

Langley Dyke

Round Hou

Limpenhoe
Marshes

Langley Marshes

Limpenhoe
Hill

River Yare

Reedham Quay

02

57

Langley
Street

Hardley
Marshes

Hardley Dyke

Hardley
Street

Norton
Staithe

REEDHAM
FERRY

Hardley
Cross
(restored)

91

36

Boundary
Fm

37

Avenue Fm

38

39

River Chet

Norton

41

Broom Hill

Nogdam End

Hall

Hardley
Hall

Hill Ho

Carr Fm

Hardley Flood

Sand
Pit

99

VE

H E
D B
H
P

M

Chedgrave Common

Beacon
Hill 21

Heckingham

Hall

Norton
Subcourse

LODDON

Hill
Fm

High House
Fm

Craft
Plantn

North
Fm

Read's
Cross

Warren
Hills

HALES

Loddon
Hall

PH

B 1136

The Orchards

Sycamore Fm

64

Raveningham

Pockthorpe

Hales Green

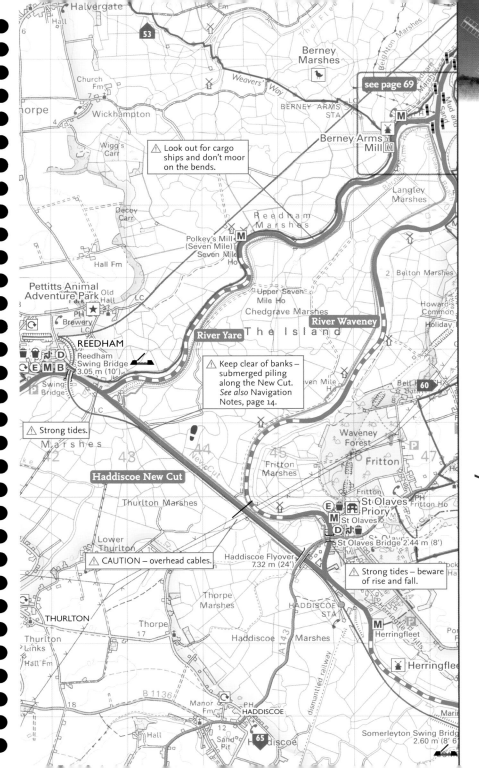

53

Halvergate

Berney
Marshes

BERNEY ARMS
STA

see page 69

Berney Arms
Mill M

M

Langley
Marshes

⚠ Look out for cargo
ships and don't moor
on the bends.

Church
Fm

Wickhampton

Wigg's
Carr

Decoy
Carr

Reedham
Marshes

Polkey's Mill M
(Seven Mile)
Seven Mile
Ho

Belton Marshes

Hall Fm

Pettitts Animal
Adventure Park
Brewery

Old
Hall

LC

Upper Seven
Mile Ho
Chedgrave Marshes

Howard's
Common

Holiday

River Waveney

River Yare The Island

REEDHAM

Reedham
Swing Bridge
3.05 m (10')

⚠ Keep clear of banks –
submerged piling
along the New Cut.
See also Navigation
Notes, page 14.

Seven Mile
Ho

Bett H 60

Swing
Bridge

LC

⚠ Strong tides.

Marshes

Waveney
Forest

Fritton

New Cut

Fritton
Marshes

Haddiscoe New Cut

Thurlton Marshes

Fritton
Ho

St Olaves
Priory
St Olaves

Fritton Ho

Lower
Thurlton

St Olaves Bridge 2.44 m (8')

⚠ CAUTION – overhead cables.

Haddiscoe Flyover
7.32 m (24')

⚠ Strong tides – beware
of rise and fall.

Thorpe
Marshes

THURLTON

Thorpe

HADDISCOE
STA

Thurlton
Links
Hall Fm

Haddiscoe Marshes

M
Herringfleet

Herringfleet

B 1136

Manor
Fm

HADDISCOE

65

Somerleyton Swing Bridge
2.60 m (8' 6

Hall

Sand
Pit

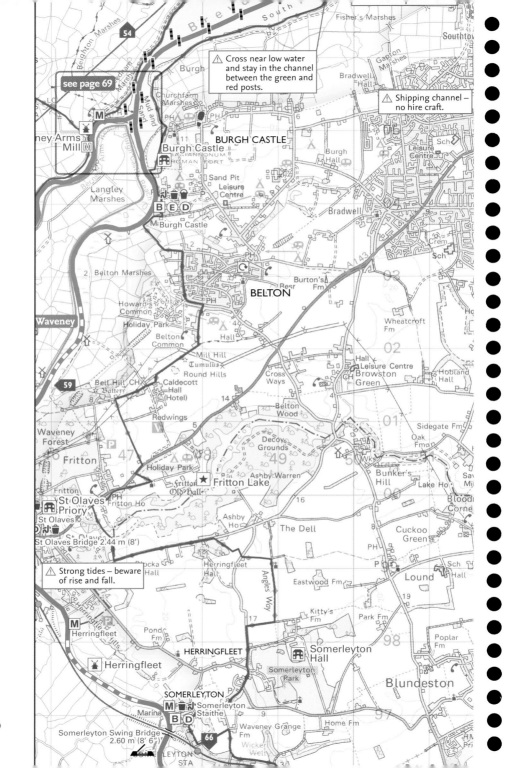

⚠ Cross near low water and stay in the channel between the green and red posts.

⚠ Shipping channel – no hire craft.

54

BURGH CASTLE

Burgh Castle

Burgh Castle
ROMAN FORT

BELTON

Waveney

59

Fritton Lake

St Olaves
Priory

St Olaves Bridge 2.44 m (8')

⚠ Strong tides – beware of rise and fall.

HERRINGFLEET

Herringfleet

Somerleyton
Hall

Blundeston

SOMERLEYTON

Somerleyton Swing Bridge
2.60 m (8' 6")

66

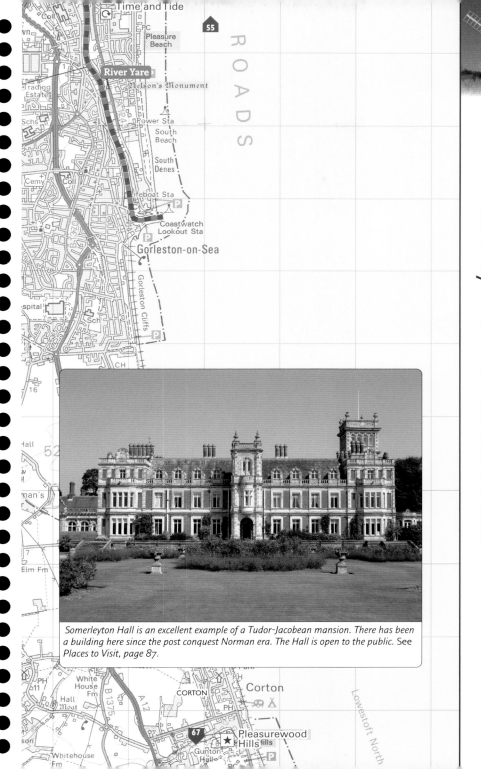

Somerleyton Hall is an excellent example of a Tudor-Jacobean mansion. There has been a building here since the post conquest Norman era. The Hall is open to the public. See Places to Visit, page 87.

Blue-tailed damselfly.

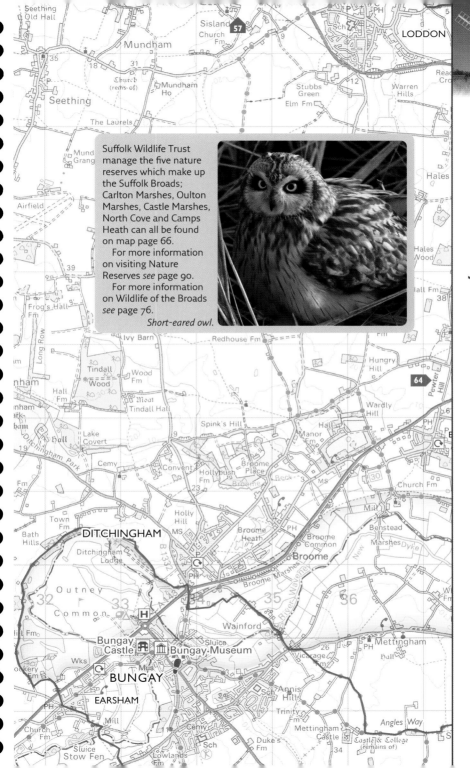

Suffolk Wildlife Trust manage the five nature reserves which make up the Suffolk Broads; Carlton Marshes, Oulton Marshes, Castle Marshes, North Cove and Camps Heath can all be found on map page 66.

For more information on visiting Nature Reserves *see* page 90.

For more information on Wildlife of the Broads *see* page 76.

Short-eared owl.

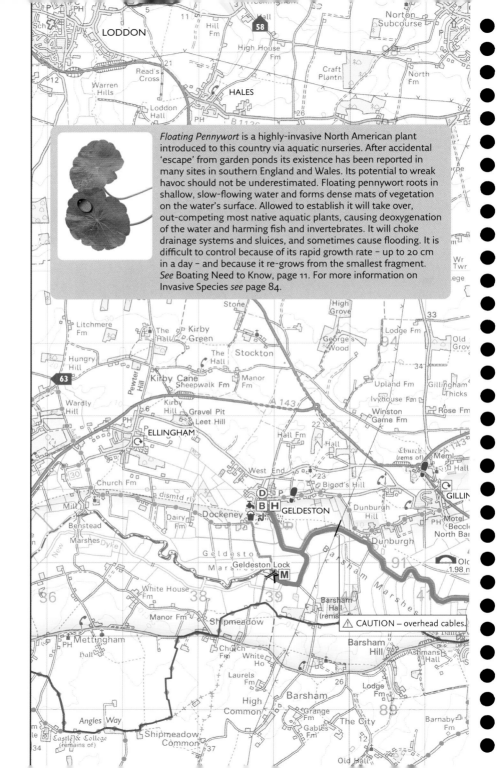

LODDON

58

High House Fm

HALES

Floating Pennywort is a highly-invasive North American plant introduced to this country via aquatic nurseries. After accidental 'escape' from garden ponds its existence has been reported in many sites in southern England and Wales. Its potential to wreak havoc should not be underestimated. Floating pennywort roots in shallow, slow-flowing water and forms dense mats of vegetation on the water's surface. Allowed to establish it will take over, out-competing most native aquatic plants, causing deoxygenation of the water and harming fish and invertebrates. It will choke drainage systems and sluices, and sometimes cause flooding. It is difficult to control because of its rapid growth rate – up to 20 cm in a day – and because it re-grows from the smallest fragment. *See* Boating Need to Know, page 11. For more information on Invasive Species *see* page 84.

ELLINGHAM

GELDESTON

Geldeston Lock

M

⚠ CAUTION – overhead cables.

Barsham Hill

Barsham

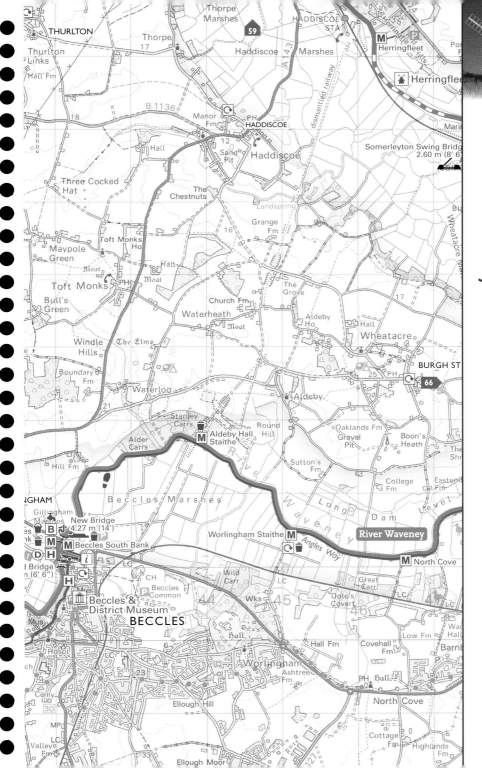

THURLTON

Thorpe
Marshes

HADDISCOE
STA

Herringfleet

Herringfleet

Thorpe
17

Haddiscoe Marshes

Thurlton
Links

Hall Fm

B 1136

Manor
Fm

PH

HADDISCOE

18

12

Somerleyton Swing Bridge
2.60 m (8' 6")

Hall

Sand
Pit

Haddiscoe

Three Cocked
Hat

The
Chestnuts

Landspring

Beck

Grange
Fm

16

Toft Monks
Ho

Maypole
Green

Moat

Hall

Moat

The
Grove

Church Fm

Toft Monks

PH

Moat

Waterheath

Aldeby
Ho

Hall

Wheatacre

Bull's
Green

Moat

BURGH ST

Windle
Hills

The Elms

25

PH

Boundary
Fm

66

Waterloo

Aldeby

21

Stanley
Carrs

Round
Hill

Oaklands Fm

Boon's
Heath

Alder
Carrs

Aldeby Hall
Staithe

Gravel
Pit

Hill Fm

Sutton's
Fm

College
Fm

Eastend
Fm

River

Beccles Marshes

Long

Dam

Level

NGHAM

Gillingham
Marshes

New Bridge
4.27 m (14')

Worlingham Staithe

Angles Way

River Waveney

Beccles South Bank

North Cove

Bridge
(6' 6")

LC

CH

Wild
Carr

LC

Great
Carr

LC

Beccles
Common

Wks

45

Dole's
Covert

46

Beccles &
District Museum

BECCLES

Hall

Hall Fm

Covehall
Fm

Low

Barn

Sch

23

Worlingham

Ashtree
Fm

PH

Hall

North Cove

Ellough Hill

Cemy

30

MP

LC

Valley
Fm

33

Ellough Moor

Cottage
Fm

Highlands
Fm

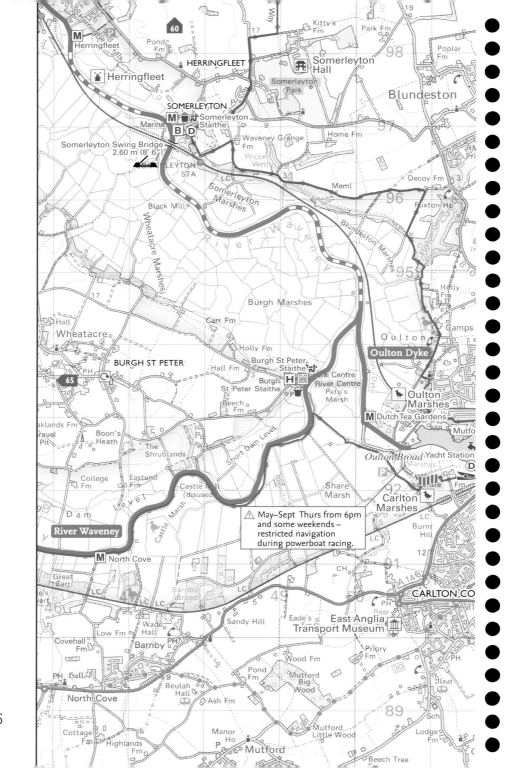

M Herringfleet   **P**

60

17   Way   Kitty's

Herringfleet Mills   Pond Fm   Park Fm

19

Poplar Fm

98

🏭 Herringfleet

HERRINGFLEET

Somerleyton Hall

Somerleyton Park

Blundeston

M 🏛 Somerleyton Staithe

SOMERLEYTON

Marina

Somerleyton Hall

9   Waveney Grange Fm

Home Fm

97

B **D**

Wicken Well

Decoy Fm   3

Somerleyton Swing Bridge 2.60 m (8' 6")

LEYTON STA

Meml

3

96

LC

Somerleyton Marshes

Flixton Ho

Black Mill

River Waveney

Blundeston Marshes

Flixton Decoy

95

Burgh Marshes

Holly Fm

Wheatacre Marshes

17   Hall

Carr Fm

Oulton

Camps

Wheatacre

Holly Fm

Oulton Dyke

Oulton Marshes

BURGH ST PETER

Hall Fm

Burgh St Peter Staithe 🏛

Oulton Dyke

65   PH

3

Burgh St Peter Staithe

H **M**

River Centre   Peto's Marsh

🦌 Oulton Marshes

M Dutch Tea Gardens

Beech Fm

Mutfo...

aklands Fm   Boon's Heath

The Shrublands

Short Dam Level

Share Marsh

Oulton Broad Yacht Station

P

D

ravel Pit

College Fm   Eastend Fm

Castle Hill (disused)

Castle Marsh

Marshes

92

🦤 Carlton Marshes

River Waveney

D a m

Level

⚠ May–Sept Thurs from 6pm and some weekends – restricted navigation during powerboat racing.

LC   Burnt Hill

91

12

M North Cove

CH   2

CARLTON CO

Great Carr

Barnby Broad

LC

e's vert

46

LC   LC

49

Eade's

East Anglia Transport Museum 🏛

PH

A146

Wade Hall

Sandy Hill

Low Fm

Covehall Fm

Barnby   PH

Priory Fm

PH

30

PH Hall

North Cove

Beulah Hall   Ash Fm

Pond Fm

Wood Fm

Mutford Big Wood

Moat

Sch

89

Cottage Fm   Highlands Fm

Manor Ho   **P**

Mutford

Mutford Little Wood

Lodge Fm

Beech Tree

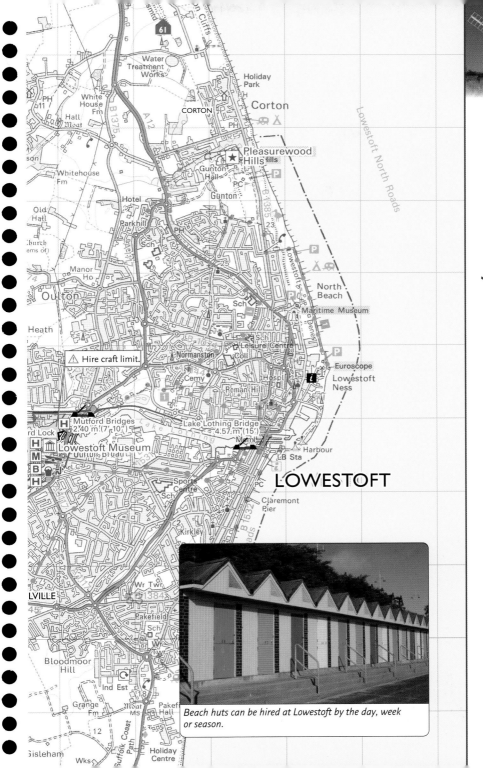

Corton

CORTON

Water
Treatment
Works

Holiday
Park

⭐ Pleasurewood
Hills Hills

Gunton
Hall

Gunton

Hotel

Parkhill

Old
Hall

Church
ems of)

Manor
Ho

Oulton

Heath

White
House
Fm

Whitehouse
Fm

Lowestoft North Roads

North
Beach

Maritime Museum

Leisure Centre

⚠ Hire craft limit.

Normanston

Cemy

Roman Hill

Euroscope
Lowestoft
Ness

Mutford Bridges
2.40 m (7'10")

Lake Lothing Bridge
4.57 m (15')

Lowestoft Museum
Oulton Broad

Lake Lothing

Harbour

LB Sta

LOWESTOFT

Sports
Centre

Claremont
Pier

Kirkley

LVILLE

Wr Twr

Pakefield

Bloodmoor
Hill

Ind Est

Grange
Fm

Pakef
Hall

Holiday
Centre

Gisleham

Wks

Beach huts can be hired at Lowestoft by the day, week or season.

67

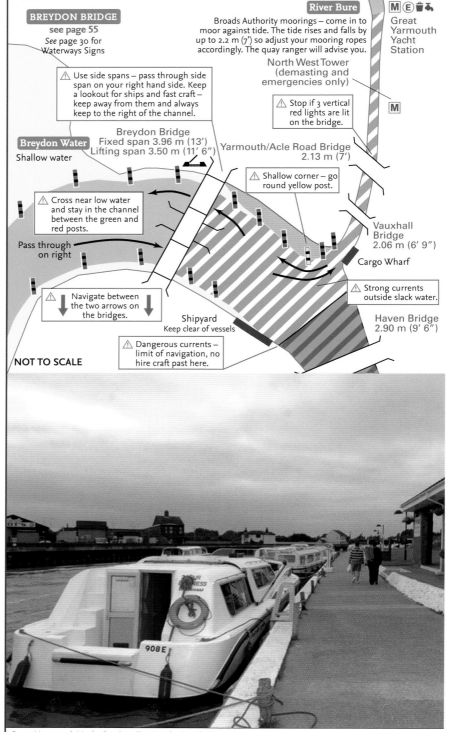

BREYDON BRIDGE
see page 55
See page 30 for Waterways Signs

River Bure

M Ⓔ 🚻 ♿

Great Yarmouth Yacht Station

Broads Authority moorings – come in to moor against tide. The tide rises and falls by up to 2.2 m (7') so adjust your mooring ropes accordingly. The quay ranger will advise you.

North West Tower (demasting and emergencies only)

⚠ Use side spans – pass through side span on your right hand side. Keep a lookout for ships and fast craft – keep away from them and always keep to the right of the channel.

⚠ Stop if 3 vertical red lights are lit on the bridge.

M

Breydon Water
Shallow water

Breydon Bridge
Fixed span 3.96 m (13')
Lifting span 3.50 m (11' 6")

Yarmouth/Acle Road Bridge 2.13 m (7')

⚠ Shallow corner – go round yellow post.

⚠ Cross near low water and stay in the channel between the green and red posts.

Vauxhall Bridge 2.06 m (6' 9")

Pass through on right

Cargo Wharf

⚠ Strong currents outside slack water.

⚠ Navigate between the two arrows on the bridges.

Shipyard
Keep clear of vessels

Haven Bridge 2.90 m (9' 6")

⚠ Dangerous currents – limit of navigation, no hire craft past here.

NOT TO SCALE

908 E

Great Yarmouth Yacht Station, Tar Works Road, Great Yarmouth (01493 842794).

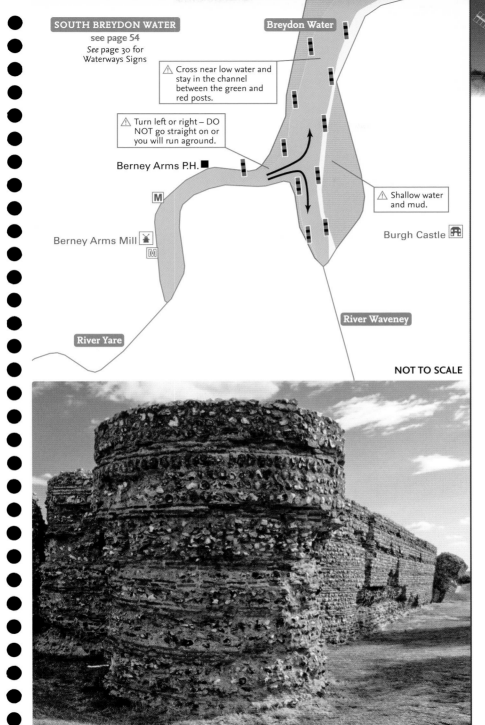

SOUTH BREYDON WATER
see page 54
See page 30 for
Waterways Signs

Breydon Water

⚠ Cross near low water and
stay in the channel
between the green and
red posts.

⚠ Turn left or right – DO
NOT go straight on or
you will run aground.

Berney Arms P.H. ◼

Ⓜ

⚠ Shallow water
and mud.

Berney Arms Mill 🎐

Ⓜ

Burgh Castle 🏠

River Waveney

River Yare

NOT TO SCALE

Burgh Castle roman fort. See Places to Visit, page 86.

	Bicycle	Boat trips	Canoes	Electric boats	Motor boats	Rowing boats	Sailing dinghies	Learn to sail (S), canoe (C) windsurf (W)
Ormesby Little Broad								
Wheelyboat Trust (page 46) ♿ *Eels Foot Inn, Eels Foot Road, Ormesby, Great Yarmouth, Norfolk NR29 3LP (01493 730342; www.wheelyboats.org)*				✓	✓			
River Ant								
Bank Dayboats (page 39) *Bank Boatyard, Staitheside, Wayford Bridge, Norwich, Norfolk NR12 9LN (01692 582457)*		✓		✓	✓			
Broadland Cycle Hire (page 44) *Ludham Bridge Stores, Johnson Street, Ludham, Norfolk NR29 5NZ (01692 630486; www.norfolkbroadscycling.co.uk)*	✓							
Ludham Bridge Boatyard (page 44) *Johnson Street, Ludham, Norfolk NR29 5NX (01692 631011; www.ludhambridgeboats.co.uk)*		✓		✓	✓	✓	✓	
Moonfleet Marine (page 39) *The Staithe, Stalham, Norwich, Norfolk NR12 9DA (01692 580288; www.moonfleetmarine.co.uk)*				✓	✓			
Nancy Oldfield Trust (page 43) ♿ *Irstead Road, Neatishead, Norwich, Norfolk NR12 8BJ (01692 630572; www.nancyoldfield.org.uk)*		✓	✓	✓	✓		✓	
Richardsons Cruisers (page 39) *The Staithe, Stalham, Norwich, Norfolk NR12 9BX (01692 581081; www.richardsonsboatingholidays.co.uk)*					✓			
Sutton Staithe Boat Hire (page 39) *Sutton Staithe, Sutton, Norfolk NR12 9QS (01692 581653; www.suttonstaitheboatyard.co.uk)*		✓			✓			
River Bure								
Barnes Brinkcraft (page 42) *Riverside Road, Wroxham, Norwich, Norfolk NR12 8UD (01603 782625; www.barnesbrinkcraft.co.uk)*		✓		✓	✓	✓		
Boulter Marine Services (page 43) *Ferry View Estate, Horning, Norfolk, Norfolk NR12 8PT (01692 630498; www.boultermarine.co.uk)*				✓	✓			

	Bicycle	Boat trips	Canoes	Electric boats	Motor boats	Rowing boats	Sailing dinghies	Learn to sail (S), canoe (C) windsurf (W)
Bridgecraft (page 53) *Acle Bridge, Acle, Norwich, Norfolk NR13 3AS (01493 750378)*				✓				
Broadland Cycle Hire (page 43) *BeWILDerwood, Horning Road, Hoveton, Norwich NR12 8JW (07887 480331; www.norfolkbroadscycling.co.uk)*	✓							
Broads Tours (page 42) ♿ *Norwich Road, Wroxham, Norfolk NR12 8RX (01603 782207; www.broads.co.uk)*		✓		✓	✓			
Eastwood-Whelpton (page 53) *Upton Yacht Station, Upton, Norwich, Norfolk NR13 6BN (01493 750430; www.eastwood-whelpton.co.uk)*						✓	✓	
Ferry Marina (page 43) ♿ *Ferry Road, Horning, Norwich, Norfolk NR12 8PS (01692 631111; www.ferryboats.co.uk)*					✓			
Fineway Launch Hire (page 42) *Fineway Leisure, The Rhond, Hoveton, Norfolk NR12 8UE (01603 782309; www.finewayleisure.co.uk)*				✓	✓			
Freedom Boating Holidays (page 43) *Ferry View Road, Horning, Norfolk NR12 8PT (01603 858453; www.freedomboatingholidays.com)*					✓			
George Smith & Sons (page 42) *The Rhond, Hoveton, Norfolk NR12 8UE (01603 782527; www.finewayleisure.co.uk)*					✓			
Horstead Centre (page 42) *(Residential outdoor centre) Rectory Road, Horstead, Norwich, Norfolk NR12 7EP (01603 737215; www.horsteadcentre.org.uk)*								✓(C)
JB Boat Sales (page 43) *106 Lower Street, Horning, Norwich, Norfolk NR12 8PF (01692 631411; wwww.jbboats.co.uk)*					✓			
King Line Cottages (page 43) ♿ *Ferry Road, Horning, Norwich, Norfolk NR12 8PS (01692 630297; www.norfolk-boats.co.uk)*				✓			✓	

River Bure (continued)

	Bicycle	Boat trips	Canoes	Electric boats	Motor boats	Rowing boats	Sailing dinghies	Learn to sail (S), canoe (C), windsurf (W)
Mississippi River Boats (page 43) ♿ *The Swan Hotel, Lower Street, Horning, Norfolk NR12 8AA (01692 630262; www.southern-comfort.co.uk)*		✓						
Norfolk Broads School of Sailing (page 53) *See Eastwood-Whelpton above (01692 582864; www.norfolksailingschool.co.uk)*								✓(S)
Norfolk Broads Yachting Company (page 43) *Southgate Yacht Station, Lower Street, Horning, Norwich, Norfolk NR12 8PF (01692 631330; www.norfolk-broads.com)*					✓	✓		
Perfecta Boats (page 43) *Lower Street, Horning, Norwich, Norfolk NR12 8AA (01692 631161)*			✓		✓	✓		
Riverside Tearooms and Stores (page 53) *The Green, Stokesby, Great Yarmouth, Norfolk NR29 3EX (01493 750470; www.stokesby.org.uk)*	✓							
Royall & Son (page 42) *Riverside Road, Hoveton, Norwich, Norfolk NR12 8UD (01603 782743)*					✓			
Russell Marine (page 44) *Fleet Lane, South Walsham, Norwich, Norfolk NR13 6ED (01603 270262; www.russellmarine.co.uk)*					✓			
Salhouse Broad (page 43) *Salhouse Road, Salhouse, Norwich, Norfolk NR13 6SD (01603 722775; www.salhousebroad.org.uk)*			✓					

River Chet

	Bicycle	Boat trips	Canoes	Electric boats	Motor boats	Rowing boats	Sailing dinghies	Learn to sail (S), canoe (C), windsurf (W)
Pacific Cruisers (page 57) *Riverside, Pits Lane, Chedgrave, Loddon, Norfolk NR14 6NQ (01508 520321; www.pacificcruisers.co.uk)*					✓			
Prestige Boats (page 57) *Bridge Street, Loddon, Norfolk NR14 6NG (01508 520353)*					✓	✓		

River Thurne

	Bicycle	Boat trips	Canoes	Electric boats	Motor boats	Rowing boats	Sailing dinghies	Learn to sail (S), canoe (C), windsurf (W)
DRL Marine Services (page 44) *Womack Staithe, Horsefen Road, Ludham, Norfolk NR29 5QG (08448 001212; www.drlmarine.com)*					✓			

CANOE HIRE

	Bicycle	Boat trips	Canoes	Electric boats	Motor boats	Rowing boats	Sailing dinghies	Learn to sail (S), canoe (C) windsurf (W)
Herbert Woods/Broads Tours (page 45) *Broads Haven Marina, Potter Heigham, Norfolk NR29 5JB (01692 670711; www.broads.co.uk)*				✓				
Hunter's Yard (page 44) *Horsefen Road, Ludham, Norfolk NR29 5QG (01692 678263; www.huntersyard.co.uk)*							✓	✓(S)
Martham Boats (page 45) *Valley Works, Cess Road, Martham, Great Yarmouth, Norfolk NR29 4RF (01493 740249; www.marthamboats.com)*		✓			✓	✓	✓	
Maycraft (page 45) *North West River Bank, Potter Heigham, Great Yarmouth, Norfolk NR29 5ND (01692 670241; www.maycraft.co.uk)*					✓			
Pheonix Fleet (page 45) *Repps Staithe Boatyard, Bridge Road, Potter Heigham, Great Yarmouth, Norfolk NR29 5JD (01692 670460; www.phoenixfleet.com)*				✓	✓			
Whispering Reeds (page 40) *Staithe Road, Hickling, Norwich, Norfolk NR12 0YW (01692 59831; www.whisperingreeds.net)*		✓			✓	✓	✓	
River Waveney								
CC Marine (page 65) *35 Northgate, Beccles, Suffolk NR34 9AU (01502 713703)*					✓			
H E Hipperson (page 65) *Hipperson Boatyard, Gillingham Dam, Beccles, Suffolk NR34 0EB (01502 712166; www.geldeston.org/hipperson.htm)*				✓	✓			
Oulton Broad Day Boats (page 67) *3–5 The Yacht Station, The Boulevard, Oulton Broad, Lowestoft, Suffolk NR33 9JU (01502 589556)*				✓	✓			
Outney Meadow Caravan Park (page 63) *Outney Meadow, Bungay, Suffolk NR35 1HG (01986 892338; www.outneymeadow.co.uk)*	✓	✓				✓		
Rowancraft (page 65) *Big Row, Geldeston, Beccles, Suffolk NR34 0LY (01508 518598; www.rowancraft.com)*				✓	✓			

	Bicycle	Boat trips	Canoes	Electric boats	Motor boats	Rowing boats	Sailing dinghies	Learn to sail (S), canoe (C) windsurf (W)
River Waveney (continued)								
The Quays (page 67) *1–4 Yacht Station, The Boulevard, Oulton Broad, Lowestoft, Suffolk NR33 9JS (01502 513087; www.thequays-oultonbroad.com)*					✓			
Waveney River Centre (page 65) *Sraithe Road, Burgh St Peter, Beccles, Suffolk NR34 0BT (01502 677343; www.waveneyrivercentre.co.uk)*	✓		✓		✓	✓		
Waveney River Tours (page 67) ♿ *Mutford Lock Bridge Road, Oulton Broad, Lowestoft, Suffolk NR33 9JU (01502 574903; www.lovelowestoft.co.uk)*		✓						
Waveney Sailability (page 67) ♿ *Oulton Broad Water Sports Centre, Nicholas Everitt Park, Oulton Broad, Lowestoft, Suffolk NR33 9JR (01502 587163; www.waveneysailability.co.uk)*								✓(S)
Waveney Stardust (page 65) ♿ *Hippersons Boatyard, Gillingham Dam, Beccles, Suffolk NR34 0EB (07817 920502; www.waveneystardust.co.uk)*		✓						
River Yare								
City Boats (page 50) ♿ *A river bus service: Griffin Lane, Thorpe St Andrew, Norwich, Norfolk NR7 0SL (01603 701701; www.cityboats.co.uk)*		✓		✓	✓			
Fencraft (page 51) *Riverside Estate, Brundall, Norwich, Norfolk NR13 5PS (01603 715011)*						✓		
The Southern Belle (page 55) ♿ *Haven Bridge, Great Yarmouth, Norfolk NR31 0GU (07906 020225; www.cyberforth.com/southernbelle)*		✓						
Whitlingham Great and Little Broads								
Whitlingham Outdoor Education Centre (page 50) *Whitlingham Lane, near Trowse, Norwich NR14 8TR (01603 632307;www.whitlinghamoec.co.uk/ www.south-norfolk.gov.uk)*	✓		✓				✓	✓(S) (C) (W)

Near the Rivers Bure and Thurne

Clippesby Hall (page 45)
*Clippesby, Norfolk NR29 3BL (01493 367800;
www.clippesby.com)*

Around the Norfolk Broads

The Canoe Man provides canoe hire, training and
guided canoe trails through the Broads.
*Contact: 102 College Road, Norwich, Norfolk NR2 3JN
(01603 499177; www.thecanoeman.co.uk)*

Boat booking agencies

Blakes Holiday Boating
*Contact: Spring Mill, Stoneybank Road, Earby,
Barnoldswick, Lancashire BB94 0AA
(08702 202498; www.blakes.co.uk)*

Hoseasons Boating Holidays
*Contact: Lowestoft, Suffolk NR32 2LW (01502
502588; www.hoseasons.co.uk/boat-holidays/)*

Waterways Holidays
*Contact: 47 Station Road, Aldershot, Hampshire
GU11 1BA (0845 127 1020)*

Independent boatyards

As well as the booking agencies, these independent
boatyards offer boating holidays on the Broads:
Freedom Boating Holidays *Ferry View Road, Horning,
Norfolk NR12 8PT (01603 858453;
www.freedomboatingholidays.com)*

Maffett Cruisers *Pits Lane, Chedgrave, Loddon,
Norwich, Norfolk NR14 6NQ (01508 520344;
www.maffett-cruisers.com)*

Posh Boats *Church Hill, Saxlingham Nethergate,
Norfolk NR15 1TD (01508 499167;
www.poshboats.co.uk)*

And also the following, all found in the listings
above: Eastwood-Whelpton, George Smith & Sons,
Hunter's Yard, Martham Boats, Norfolk Broads
Yachting Company, Pacific Cruisers.

♿ Wheelchair accessible – please contact the
companies for further information.

	Bicycle	Boat trips	Canoes	Electric boats	Motor boats	Rowing boats	Sailing dinghies	Learn to sail (S), canoe (C), windsurf (W)
Clippesby Hall	✓							
The Canoe Man			✓					✓(C)
Blakes Holiday Boating				✓	✓			
Hoseasons Boating Holidays				✓				
Waterways Holidays				✓	✓			

The Broads contain a variety of differing habitats, supporting diverse species of wildlife. This unique wetland of rivers and broads is surrounded by semi-natural habitats: fen, carr woodland and grazing marsh.

Fen.

There is a natural change (if allowed to take place) from an area of open water to woodland. Fen is the first stage in this succession: waterlogged areas dominated by reeds, rushes and sedges. In spite of a significant loss of fen to woodland in the Broads since the early 19th century, there are about 1,700 ha (4,200 acres) of open fen – the largest expanses of species-rich fen in lowland Britain.

Carr woodland.

When fen is left unmanaged, small shrubs and trees start to grow, creating carr woodland. There are around 3,000 ha (7,413 acres) of woodland and scrub in the Broads, a third of which has developed during the past 50 years or so. Mature carr woodland is the most valuable: a tangle of woody species, shade-tolerant and low growing plants such as alder, sallow and birch trees, guelder rose, buckthorn, dog rose and brambles, ferns, mosses, lichen and fungi.

Grazing marsh.

The Broads have had areas of grazing marsh since the 13th century, when sheep were grazed and marsh reclamation started. This trend continued through to the 20th century, at each stage drainage becoming more efficient and flooding become rarer. Today the grazing marshes support internationally and nationally important populations of wintering wildfowl, as well as raptors and breeding waders, and a host of invertebrate and plant communities. Skylarks are numerous, together with yellow wagtails and meadow pipits. Barn owls, short-eared owls, kestrels and occasionally marsh harriers feed on the abundant supply of small mammals.

The following pages describe just a small selection of the wildlife to be seen in the Broads. Take a good guide with you when you visit the area (such as one of the Collins wildlife guides). Spend some time at one of the nature reserves (*see* Places to Visit, page 90), or contact the Broads Authority (*see* page 24) for details of activities designed to introduce visitors to the unique natural environment of the Broads. At the end of the chapter, we have included a list of some invasive species – the non-native creatures and plants that threaten the natural and native environment.

BIRDS *The Broads are renowned for many different bird species.*

Bearded tit The bearded tit is one of several birds particularly associated with the Broads. It is an elusive species living in dense reedbeds where it feeds on insects, especially the larvae of moths, also spiders and seeds. It is usually seen in small groups, clambering up the reeds or flying, one after the other. Its call is a loud *ching-ching*. In some years, when numbers have built up, it 'erupts' and spreads to new areas. However, a severe winter can drastically reduce populations. Nests are built among the reeds. The bearded tit grows to 16–17 cm (6–6.5 inches) and has a long tail and mainly sandy-brown plumage; the male has a blue-grey head and conspicuous black 'moustaches'.

Bewick's swan The smallest British swan – it is a winter visitor between October and March from Siberian breeding grounds. The adults are pure white with a black and yellow bill, triangular in profile and barely reaching the nostrils. Juveniles have pinkish buff plumage and a pinkish bill: they arrive in Britain and remain together as family parties among larger flocks. Most birds return to traditional wintering sites and internationally important flocks of Bewick's swans have been recorded on Breydon Water.

Bittern The bittern is another bird species especially associated with the Broads. Deterioration of water quality and fenland habitat during the 20th century saw a sharp decline in numbers, but the Broads authority have been active in restoring habitats suitable for the bittern. The birds are seldom seen on account of their retiring nature and excellent camouflage afforded by the streaked buffish brown plumage in their favoured reedbed habitat. Their presence is often indicated by the male's loud booming call, uttered at dusk and through the night from April to June. When seen resting, the bird has a dumpy, hunched appearance. If alarmed, however, it adopts an upright, sky-pointing posture with its neck outstretched and the dagger-like bill held vertically. It will occasionally be seen briefly in flight, flying low over the tops of reeds on broad, rounded wings, with legs trailing. It grows to 70–80 cm (27.5–31.5 inches) and feeds mainly on fish and amphibians, but will take small waterside mammals too.

Long-tailed tit A charming resident of woods, heaths and hedgerows, feeding flocks resemble animated feather dusters. Outside the breeding season, the birds roost communally. These tits have a tiny, almost spherical body and a very long tail, with a small, stubby bill. Their plumage can look black and white, but at close range they have a pinkish wash to the underparts and are pinkish buff on the back. Their beautiful domed nests are built of moss, lichen and spider's webs.

Marsh harrier Another bird particularly connected with the Broads area and one that has made a successful comeback in recent times thanks to improved fen management. This rare bird is associated with wetlands, particularly extensive reedbeds. It flies at a slow speed just above the tops of the reeds, occasionally stalling to drop on prey. It is long-winged, with a wingspan of 110–125 cm (43–49 inches), and long-tailed. The male is reddish brown except for its blue-grey head and grey, unbarred tail; in flight, it has grey and reddish brown areas on the wings and black wingtips. The female is dark brown, except for a pale leading edge to the wing, and pale cap and chin. The nest is a pile of reeds and sticks on marshy ground.

Reed warbler As the name suggests, almost always associated with reedbeds. A common visitor from May–August. These singing birds 12–13 cm (5 inches) long, clamber up reeds or occasionally use bushes to deliver grating, chattering song that includes some mimetic elements. They have rather nondescript sandy-brown upperparts, paler underparts and dark legs. Nests are woven and cup-shaped, attached to upright reed stems. Reed warblers feed on insects.

Treecreeper A woodland bird, unobtrusive and easily overlooked as it creeps like a mouse up tree-trunks and larger branches. It typically feeds by spiralling round and up a tree, then dropping down to the base of an adjacent trunk to repeat the process – it will be searching for insects and spiders and, in winter, some seeds. It has streaked brown upperparts, pale underparts and a needle-like, downcurved bill, and is 12–13 cm (5 inches) long. The spiky tail is used as support when climbing. Its nest is built in a crevice, often behind loose bark.

Wigeon A scarce breeding species but locally common winter visitor to Britain. Breydon Water shelters nationally important wintering flocks. The male has an orange-red head with yellow forehead, pinkish breast and otherwise finely marked, grey plumage, with a characteristic black and white stern. In flight, the male has a bold white wing patch. The reddish brown female is best told by association with the male. The male's *wheeoo* call is evocative of winter estuaries.

Willow tit An inhabitant of the Broads' swampy carr woodland. It is similar in appearance to the marsh tit and is best identified by its nasal *tchay tchay tchay* call. The pale patch on its wing is not always distinguishable. It has a large head, pale wing-panel, dull black crown and a square-ended tail and is around 11–12 cm (4–5 inches) long. Its bill is small and black. The usual nest site is a hole excavated in a rotten tree stump. Willow tits feed on insects and seeds.

FISH *The Broads support a wide variety of fish species and offer wonderful opportunities for fishing (see Angling, page 20).*

Bream A large 80 cm (31.5 inches) long, deep-bodied fish found in slow-moving rivers and brackish waters – large shoals are found throughout the Broads area. The fish feeds on invertebrates sucked from mud on the river bottom forming 'bream pits'. Bream are grey-brown above, silvery below on their sides. Larger fish may have a bronze tinge. They breed between April and June, spawning at night in shallow waters over vegetation such as weeds. Up to 340,000 yellowish eggs are laid and these hatch after about two weeks.

Perch A popular sport fish making a comeback to the waters of the Broads after a disease that decimated them during the 1970s. Perch inhabit lakes and slow rivers, often sheltering near roots, under overhanging trees, in deep reeds or under permanent moorings. They are dark green above, lighter below, with lateral lines on their sides. The two prominent dorsal fins are close together, with a dark blotch at the base of the first dorsal fin. The pelvic and anal fins are reddish. They grow to around 50 cm (19.5 inches). Spawning in late April–May, up to 200,000 pale yellowish eggs are laid over weed, appearing as long white strands.

Pike Commonplace throughout the Broads, this delicate species requires specialist tackle and skillful handling, in spite of its ferocious looks. It is a large predator – males averaging 90 cm (35.5 inches) long, females 150 cm (59 inches) – with a long snout and jaws and powerful teeth. Coloured olive green above and white or yellow below. The distinctive patterns on the sides are unique to larger specimens. The pike hunts alone, among vegetation, waiting motionless to pounce on prey: usually other fish but sometimes small mammals and young water birds. Spawning takes places in spring. Up to 500,000 tiny, yellowish eggs, in clusters of oil droplets are laid on vegetation in shallow water, hatching after 10–15 days.

Rudd Still common in the Broads waters, despite increasing scarcity throughout other parts of the country. Rudd are a shoal fish, preferring thick, reedy lakes and slow rivers. Similar in appearance to the roach, the rudd has a deep, flat-sided body, around 35–40 cm (14–16 inches), with its dorsal fin far back, and a jutting bottom jaw. Its back is coloured bluish-green, fading to a deep gold at the flank, and is silvery-white underneath. The fins are a deep orange; eyes are yellow-orange. Spawning takes place April–June. The eggs laid in large mats attached to reed stems and hatch after about seven days.

Wildlife of the Broads

79

INSECTS

The increasingly good condition of the water in the Broads has lead to a much improved biodiversity, leading to more plants and insects, which in turn has led to an increased number of bird and fish species.

Comma butterfly Recognised by its distinctive ragged-edged wings, span 45 mm (2 inches) and smoky-brown underwings, with a white 'comma' mark; the upperwings are orange-brown with dark markings. It is double-brooded and hibernates. Flies March–September. The caterpillars feed on common nettle, elm and hops.

Common darter One of the most common dragonflies in England and Wales. The mature male has a blood-red abdomen, although in immature males and females this is orange-brown. The nymph is found among pondweed and debris. It frequently rests on the ground, but also uses perches. The common darter flies June–late autumn, often the latest flying species of dragonfly.

Banded demoiselle An attractive damselfly, often found resting among waterside vegetation. The males can be seen in small fluttering groups hovering over water while the flight of the female is rather feeble. They favour clean streams where the nymphs live partly buried in muddy sediment. The male has a blue body with a metallic sheen, the smoky wings show a conspicuous blue 'thumbprint' mark. The female has a green body with a metallic sheen and greenish brown wings. They grow to around 45 mm (2 inches) long. Flies May–August.

Glow worm The grub-like, wingless females, 14 mm (0.5 inches) long, may be located after dark by a greenish light emitted from the underside of tip to abdomen. This serves to attract winged males. The females will usually climb up grass stems and their luminosity ceases temporarily if they are disturbed. The adults do not feed, but the larvae, which can also emit light, eat snails. They may be found in meadows and along forest rides and verges.

Norfolk hawker dragonfly A rarity, one of two brown hawker dragonflies found in the United Kingdom, and restricted to the Broads fens and grazing marshes – it is the emblem of the Broads Authority. It has clear, untinted wings, green eyes and a yellow triangular mark on the second abdominal segment. Flies mainly June–July, although it can sometimes be seen through to early August.

Swallowtail butterfly Britain's largest butterfly, with a wingspan of around 70 mm (3.75 inches), unmistakable and rare, now confined to the wetlands of the Broads. Ragged robin and meadow thistle, found growing in the Broads fens, provide a vital food source, and milk parsley provides food for the caterpillars. The swallowtail flies between May and June, and again in August. Hickling Broad is a good place to look for the swallowtail, as is Strumpshaw Fen and How Hill (*see* Places to Visit, page 86).

MAMMALS *The various differing habitats of the Broads provide good conditions for many mammals.*

Brown hare Formerly widespread and common, but has declined in many areas, in part due to persecution but also because of changes in land use. They are found in the Broads area, particularly on the grazing marshes. The brown hare is larger, longer legged and has longer, black-tipped ears than a rabbit. The males chase and box one another in spring.

Daubenton's bat A medium-sized bat with comparatively short ears. It is frequently associated with water and seen flying low over lakes, ponds and canals just as dusk is falling. It also feeds along woodland rides. Chirps can be heard by those with good hearing. It roosts in summer, sometimes in colonies, in hollow trees and tunnel entrances. In winter it hibernates.

Harvest mouse Britain's smallest rodent. It has orange-brown fur and is mainly nocturnal. Its presence is usually indicated by tennis ball-sized nests of woven grasses constructed among plant stems. The prehensile tail is almost as long as its body and is used when climbing among plant stems.

Otter The river corridors of the Broads are an important habit for otters and the Broads Authority have strict operating procedures to avoid disturbing them. The otter is superbly adapted to an amphibious lifestyle and its dives may last for several minutes. It feeds mainly on fish. Persecution from fishing interests, hunting and habitat destruction have caused a serious decline in numbers, but otters are increasingly seen in the Broads, following reintroduction efforts by the Otter Trust at Earsham.

Red deer An imposing animal and Britain's largest native land mammal. The male is larger that the female and has well developed, branching antlers. These are shed each February, reappear in the spring and become larger with each successive season. The summer coat is reddish brown but appears more grey-brown in winter; the underparts and rump are lighter. Red deer live in separate sex herds for much of the year and spend much of the daytime resting or wallowing in mud. They are most active from dusk to dawn. The annual autumn rut is accompanied by roaring, bellowing sounds from the stags.

Water vole Found in the dykes within the Broads, but have become rather scare in other areas due to habitat loss and predation by mink. These charming waterside mammals will dive into the water if danger threatens – they swim well both on the water's surface and underwater. The burrow complex usually has at least one submerged entrance. They grow to 18–22 cm (7–8.5 inches) long.

PLANTS
The Broads is one of the most wildlife-rich areas of all the country's national parks – the fens alone support more than 250 plant species.

Crested buckler fern Found in wet heaths, marshes and fens. Fronds are narrow and 2-times pinnately divided, arranged in a ladder-like pattern, growing up to 1 m (3 feet) tall.

Cross-leaved heath A downy, grey-green undershrub, growing up to 30 cm (12 inches) in height. It favours damp, acid soils, typical of boggy-margins on heaths and moors, and is widespread on the fens. The narrow leaves are in whorls of four along the stems. Pink flowers 5–6 cm (2 inches) long, are borne in terminal clusters from June–October.

Early marsh-orchid Found in damp meadows, often on calcareous soils but also acid conditions, growing up to 60 cm (23.5 inches) tall. The leaves are unmarked, yellowish green and narrow-lanceolate. The flowers are usually flesh-pink but can range from almost white to purple. The three-lobed flower lip is strongly reflexed along the mid-line. Flowers are borne on open spikes, May–June.

Grey willow Also known as grey sallow, this tree is named for the ash-coloured hairs which densely cover the young twigs and the underside of the broad oval leaves. The leaves develop inrolled margins with age. It is common to wet habitats and forms a broad crown in mature specimens. The catkins appear before the leaves, between March and April.

Guelder rose This shrub, or small tree, grows up to 4 m (13 feet) high. The leaves are divided into five, irregularly-toothed lobes. Flowers appear June–July in flat-topped heads, the inner ones much smaller then the outer ones. The berries are red.

Ragged robin A widespread and common perennial of damp meadows, marshes and the Broads fens. The narrow, grass-like leaves are rough, the upper ones in opposite pairs. The delicate-looking flowers comprise five pink petals each of which is divided into four lobes and they appear May–July. Ragged robin is an important food source for the swallowtail butterfly.

Meadow thistle A perennial of damp meadows, locally common in south and central England, Wales and Ireland, and found in the Broads fens, where it provides food for the swallowtail butterfly. The stem is unwinged, downy and ridged. Oval, toothed leaves are green and hairy above and white cottony below. The flower heads, 20–25 mm (1 inch) across, appear between June and July – reddish-purple florets and darker bracts on solitary heads.

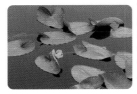

Yellow water lily Water plant with oval, floating leaves, 20–30 cm (8–12 inches) across. Widespread and locally common. This water lily favours still or slow-moving water and roots in mud in the shallows. The flowers, carried on stalks, are 50–60 cm (19.5–23.5 inches) across and appear June–September.

INVASIVE SPECIES

There is a real and serious threat to both the environment and our native wildlife from non-native species. In recent years certain invasive non-native species have become a problem in and alongside the UK's canals and rivers. Within the Broads, as with other inland waterways, the non-native species cause extensive damage by changing natural habitats, making them unsuitable for local species and, sometimes, displacing them entirely.

Problem-causing plants include Japanese knotweed (see below), Himalayan balsam and giant hogweed. They quickly come to dominate riverbanks and exclude the native plants. Floating pennywort (see page 64), water fern and parrot's feather are water plants which choke drains and rivers, causing problems to navigation, nature conservation and flood management. The American signal crayfish carry a disease which kills our native white-clawed crayfish, and American mink threaten the Broads' water vole population. Foreign molluscs, such as the zebra mussel and the Asiatic clam block pipework and water intakes and have a negative impact on native mussels.

The Broads Authority monitors known problem sites and actively keeps a look out for fresh infestations. Please report any sightings of these or other non-native species to the Broads Authority or the Environment Agency (for contact details see page 24). For more information, visit the website of the GB Non-Native Species Secretariat at www.nonnativespecies.org.

American mink An unwelcome alien which has become established after escaping from fur farms during the past few decades and is now established throughout the UK. The dark brown fur makes confusion with the otter possible, but the mink's smaller size 30–47 cm (12–18.5 inches), slimmer build and proportionally shorter tail help distinguish it. The American mink usually has white patches on its chin and throat, and small amounts of white fur may be present on the upper lip. It is invariably associated with water, particularly rivers and lakes, where it feeds on water birds, fish and waterside small mammals – it poses significant threat to the water vole population in the Broads.

Hickling Broad.

Himalayan balsam was introduced from the Himalayas as a garden plant in the early 19th century. It is widely naturalised along river banks and on damp wasteground. It has small, explosive seeds, by which it easily spreads. The plant aggressively out-grows native species in ecologically sensitive areas, especially on river banks, where it can impede the flow of water at times of high rain flow, increasing the likelihood of flooding. During winter this annual dies back, leaving the bare river banks more susceptible to erosion. Himalayan balsam grows up to 2 m (6.5 feet) tall. The upright, reddish stems carry leaves in whorls of three or opposite pairs. Pink/purple flowers, 30–40 mm (1–1.5 inches) long, appear July–October.

Japanese knotweed is fast growing, reaching more than 3 m (10 feet) in height. It is quick to colonise riverbanks, roadsides and other wayside places. Large, triangular leaves are borne on red, zigzag stems. Loose spikes of white flowers arise from leaf bases and appear between August and October. Once established, populations are extremely persistent, can survive severe floods and are difficult and expensive to eradicate.

Zebra mussels are native to south east Russia. The female mussels can produce a million eggs per season, and dense colonies quickly become established which can contain hundreds of thousands of individuals. The distinctively striped mussels grow to around 30–50 mm (1–2 inches). Unlike our native mussels which burrow in sediment, the zebra mussels attach themselves to submerged hard surfaces such as pipework, masonry, lock gates and posts, and rapidly filter out nutrients from the water.

There are many wonderful places to visit in the Broads, including restored windmills, ancient buildings, beautiful gardens and, of course, the Broads themselves. Listed below is just a selection – for more ideas on days out and places to go, visit one of the Broads Authority Information Centres (*see* Where to Get More Information, page 24). Please note that opening times are subject to change and it is always advisable to check in advance. Note that some post codes, particularly those given for nature reserves and the like, will only be the **nearest** post code to the location.

The Broads is a wetland, so for some visits you may need waterproof shoes or boots. In summer don't forget sunscreen and a sun hat. Insect repellent may be useful, especially when close to the water.

HISTORIC BUILDINGS

Bungay Castle (page 63) *Cross Street, Bungay, Suffolk NR35 1DZ (01986 896156; www.bungay-suffolk.co.uk). The original Norman keep was completed in 1165. A second castle was built in 1294 and this construction provided the town with the huge protective flint walls and the twin towers of the gatehouse, which can be seen today. Tourist information and visitor centre, café. Open all year, daily 10.00–16.00; occasional evening openings, telephone for details. Nominal charge.*

Burgh Castle (page 60) *At the far western end of Breydon Water, 5 km (3 miles) west of Great Yarmouth, Norfolk NR31 9QG (www.english-heritage.org.uk/ www.norarchtrust.org.uk). In a striking position, with panoramic views over Breydon Water. The castle comprises the imposing flint walls of a 3rd-century Roman fort, built to defend the coast from Saxon raiders. The adjacent reed beds attract many different birds, including bearded tits, reed and sedge warblers. Access at all reasonable times. Free.*

The spire and roof of Norwich Cathedral.

Caister Roman Site (page 55) *Near Caister-on-Sea, 5 km (3 miles) north of Great Yarmouth, Norfolk NR30 5QZ (0870 333 1181; www.english-heritage.org.uk; www.norarchtrust.org.uk). Remains of a Roman Saxon shore fort, including foundations and sections of wall and ditch. The fort was constructed around AD 200 and occupied until the end of the 4th century. Well-behaved dogs welcome. Access at all reasonable times. Free.*

Norwich Castle, Museum and Art Gallery (page 49) *Castle Meadow, Norwich, Norfolk NR1 3JU (01603 493625; www.museums.norfolk.gov.uk). Built by the Normans as a royal palace and used as prison from the 14th-century. Today the castle contains fine collections of art, archaeology and natural history, and the world's largest collection of ceramic teapots. Visitors can also discover what life was like in the Norman keep. Shop and café. Wheelchair access and disabled toilet. Open all year, Mon–Fri 10.00–16.30, Sat until 17.00, Sun 13.00–17.00; school holidays Mon–Sat until 17.30; Sun 13.00–17.00. Charge.*

Norwich Cathedral (page 49) *The Close, Norwich, Norfolk NR1 4DH (01603 218300; www.cathedral.org.uk). Founded in 1096 and built in the Romanesque style. It has* been voted Norfolk's most loved building. The cathedral has the second tallest spire and the largest monastic cloisters in England, many of the buildings retaining their medieval origins. The herb garden is a pleasant, quiet space. Restaurant/coffee shop. Wheelchair access and disabled toilet. *Cathedral open daily 07.30–18.00; restaurant Mon–Sat 10.00–17.00, Sun 11.00–17.00; garden, daily 09.00–17.00; shop Mon–Sat 09.15–17.00, Sun 11.45–15.30. Free.*

St Benet's Abbey (page 44) *Most easily accessed by boat. By car or foot, access via a farm lane (often muddy) near Ludham Hall Farm, on the edge of the River Bure, Norfolk NR29 5NU (www.norfarchtrust.org.uk).* An isolated spot on an island called Cow Holm, beside the River Bure. A derelict 18th-century windmill and the ruins of a Benedictine monastery. *Access at all reasonable times. Free.*

St Helen's Church, Ranworth (page 43) *Ranworth, Norfolk NR13 6HT (01603 270263; www.broadsideparishes.org.uk).* Built in 1370 on the site of a Saxon church. St Helen's is known as the 'Cathedral of the Broads' and contains some wonderful treasures, including an extensive 15th-century painted rood screen and the Ranworth Antiphonal, a beautifully illuminated 15th-century service book. Climb the 30.5 m (100 feet) Ranworth tower for panoramic views of the broads. Visitor centre (small charge) and tearoom. *Open daily during daylight hours. Free.*

St Olaves Priory (page 59) *9 km (5.5 miles) south west of Great Yarmouth, near Haddiscoe, Norfolk NR31 9HE (01493 488609; www.english-heritage.org.uk).* The rare remains of a 14th-century Augustinian priory, later a cottage occupied until 1902, located near the bridge on the banks of the River Waveney. Key available from Priory House (*see* telephone number above). Dogs on leads and only in restricted areas. *Access at all reasonable times. Free.*

Somerleyton Hall (page 60) *Lowestoft, Suffolk NR32 5QQ (01502 734901; www.somerleyton.co.uk).* Widely regarded as one of the best examples of a Tudor-Jacobean manor house, rebuilt in 1844 and still in use as a family home. Gardens, maze and miniature railway. All areas of the hall and gardens are wheelchair accessible. Wheelchairs available for visitors' use. Disabled toilet. Part of the Somerleyton Estate, which also includes Fritton Lake (*see* page 94). *Open Apr–Oct, Thu and Sun; mid-Jul–Sep, also Tue and Wed; and B Hols: gardens and tearoom 10.00–17.00, hall 11.30–15.30. Charge.*

Waxham Great Barn (page 40) *Sea Palling, Norfolk NR12 0DY (01603 222705; www.english-heritage.org.uk).* A Grade I listed barn, originally constructed in the late 16th century, with later additions. Much of the building material was reused from dissolved monasteries. It is the largest barn in Norfolk, at almost 55 m (180 feet) long. Café. Wheelchair access (gravel path) and disabled toilet. *Open May–Oct, 10.30–16.30 (telephone to confirm times). Charge for adults only.*

St Helen's Church, Ranworth.

⚙ MILLS AND WIND PUMPS

Berney Arms Mill (page 54) *On the north bank of the River Yare, 5.5 km (3.5 miles) north east of Reedham, Norfolk NR30 1SB (01493 857900; www.english-heritage. org.uk). Access by boat trips from Haven Bridge, Great Yarmouth; by train from Berney Arms Station; footpaths from Halverage and Great Yarmouth.* The tallest wind pump in the country, giving wonderful views of the marshes. Built to grind a constituent of cement and in use until 1951. *Open Jul–Aug, Mon 11.30 and 14.15, telephone to confirm times. Charge.*

Herringfleet (page 60) *South west of Herringfleet church, on the River Waveney, Suffolk NR32 5QT. Can be reached via a footpath from the B1074 (01473 264755; www.enjoyengland.com).* Constructed in the early 19th-century, the mill was in use until around 1956 and is the only full-sized working smock drainage mill in the Broads. *Telephone for opening times.*

Horsey Wind Pump (page 45) *Horsey, Great Yarmouth, Norfolk NR29 4EF (01263 740241; www.nationaltrust.org.uk).* A four-storey wind pump, built in 1912, located in a great area for birdwatching. Fine views across the Broads. Wheelchair accessible nature garden, including raised ponds and

Beccles & District Museum.

wildflower meadow. Disabled toilet. *Open Apr–Sep, daily 10.00–17.00; also Mar, Sat–Sun and Sep–mid-Oct Wed–Sun; telephone to confirm. Charge.*

Stracey Arms Wind Pump (page 54) *Beside the River Bure, on A47 between Acle and Great Yarmouth, Norfolk NR13 3QE (01603 222705; ww.norfolkwindmills.co.uk).* A wind pump, originally built in 1883. Also photographic exhibition. Tearoom and shop. Free moorings. *Open Easter–Sep, daily 09.00–20.00. Charge.*

Thurne Dyke (page 44) *On the River Thurne. The Staithe, Thurne, Great Yarmouth, Norfolk NR29 3BU (01692 672155; www.norfolkwindmills.co.uk).* A white-painted brick tower mill, built in 1820 as a two-storey mill, with a third storey added later. The mill is complete with its sails and internal machinery. *Open Apr–Sep, second and fourth Sun in each month 14.00–17.00, or by appointment. Telephone for details. Charge.*

🏛 MUSEUMS

Beccles & District Museum (page 65) *Leman House, Ballygate, Beccles, Suffolk NR34 9ND (01502 715722; www.becclesmuseum.org.uk).* Housed in a magnificent 16th-century building, built in the early 1500s and restored and modernised in the 1760s. This local and natural history museum is manned entirely by unpaid volunteers. Displays range from a few Iron Age and Roman items to a large number of Victorian artifacts, including a scale model of 1854 Beccles. Large historical photographic collection of local people and places and a growing historical database of Beccles clock makers. Wheelchair access and disabled toilet. *Open Easter–Oct, Tue–Sun and Bank Holiday Mons 14.15– 17.00. Will open outside normal hours for groups and school visits: enquire in advance. Free (donation appreciated).*

Bungay Museum (page 63) *Waveney District Council Office, Broad Street, Bungay, Suffolk NR35 1EE (01986 892176; www.bungay-suffolk.co.uk).* Local history museum currently housed on the first floor of the Waveney District Council office. The collections include a large number of coins and medals, archaeological specimens, photographs, displays on local printing works, costume and textiles, decorative and applied art and social history. *Open all year, Mon–Fri 09.30–13.00 and 14.00–16.00 (closed B Hols). Nominal charge for adults, children free.*

Caister Castle and Car Collection (page 55) *Castle Lane, Caister-on-Sea, Great Yarmouth, Norfolk NR30 5SN (01572 787649; www.caistercastle.co.uk).* A ruined, moated 15th-century castle, originally commissioned in 1432. The 27.5 m (90 feet) tower is intact and visitors can climb it for magnificent views. The car collection includes many rare cars and motorbikes. Also bicycles, horse-drawn vehicles and pedal cars. Picnic area, café, woodland walk. Wheelchair access and disabled toilet. *Open May–Sep, Sun–Fri 10.00–16.30. Charge (children under 5 free).*

East Anglia Transport Museum (page 66) *Chapel Road, Carlton Colville, Lowestoft, Suffolk NR33 8BL (01502 518459; www.eatm.org.uk).* A museum of street transport, based around a re-created street scene of houses and shops,

with vintage commercial vehicles, buses, trams and trolley buses, cars and a light railway. Visitors can take rides on different vehicles. Exhibition halls. Regular special events. Picnic area, woodland walk, gift shop and tearooms. Well-behaved dogs welcome. Wheelchair access to many buildings, although much of the museum site has uneven terrain; wheelchair accessible tram and train – confirm availability in advance. Disabled toilet.
Open Apr–Sep, daily during school holidays. Telephone or visit website to confirm times. Charge.

Lowestoft Museum (page 67) *Broad House, Nicholas Everitt Park, Oulton Broad, Lowestoft, Suffolk NR33 9JR (01502 511457; www.lowestoftmuseum.org).*

RAF Air Defence Radar Museum (page 43) *RAF Neatishead, near Horning, Norwich, Norfolk NR12 8YB (01692 631485; www.radarmuseum.co.uk).* An award-winning museum illustrating the history and development of air defence radar since its invention in 1935, located on an operational RAF base. Visitors can explore the history and development of detection, air intelligence photography, radar and air battle management, from the 1930s through to today's computer technology. Lots of hands-on exhibits and re-created operation's room. Free guided tours, souvenir shop, café and picnic areas. Wheelchair access. *Open Apr–Oct, Tue and Thu 10.00–17.00; also the second Sat of the month all year, and B Hol Mons. Charge (children under 13 free).*

Stalham Old Firehouse Museum (page 39) *Corner of St Mary's churchyard, High Street, Stalham, Norwich, Norfolk NR12 9BB (01692 582391; www.northnorfolk.org).* Photographs, artefacts and a 1902 horse-drawn fire engine housed in the country's second oldest firehouse. Disabled access. *Open Easter–Sep, Tue, Thu–Fri 10.00–12.00 and 14.00–16.00 (telephone to arrange a visit outside these hours). Free (donations welcome).*

East Anglia Transport Museum.

Strumpshaw Steam Museum (page 52) *Strumpshaw, Norwich, Norfolk NR13 4HR (01603 714535; www.strumpshawsteam museum.co.uk).* Many, many steam engines, including wagons, pumps, engines, tractors, working beam engines and a Christie cinema organ. Narrow gauge railway, a 1930s fairground, countryside walks and a collection of rare breeds. Engines in steam last Sun in month. Annual steam rally end May. Tearoom and gift shop. Wheelchair access and toilet. Well-behaved dogs welcome. *Open Apr–Jun, Sun, Wed and B Hols and Jul–Oct, Sun–Fri, 10.30–15.30. Charge.*

Time and Tide (page 55) *Blackfriars Road, Great Yarmouth, Norfolk NR30 3BX (01493 743930; www.museums.norfolk.gov.uk).* Award-winning museum housed in a converted Victorian herring-curing works. Lively exhibits describe Great Yarmouth's history and rich maritime and fishing heritage. Recreations of a Victorian fisherman's cottage, 1950s quayside and the wheelroom of a coastal drifter. Historic fishing boats and hands-on games, puzzles and children's activities. Café. Wheelchair access and toilets. *Open Apr–Oct, daily 10.00–17.00; Nov–Mar, Mon–Fri 10.00–16.00, Sat–Sun 12.00–16.00. Charge.*

Toad Hole Cottage Museum (page 44) *How Hill, Ludham, Great Yarmouth, Norfolk NR29 5PG (01692 678763; www.broads-authority.gov.uk).* Situated on a nature reserve beside the River Ant. A tiny marshman's cottage, built sometime between 1780 and 1820, illustrating a home and working life on the marshes over 100 years ago. *Open Apr–May and Oct, Mon–Fri 10.30–13.00 and 13.30–17.00, weekends 10.30–17.00; Jun–Sep, daily 09.30–18.00. Free.*

NATURE RESERVES

The many nature reserves in the Broads are mostly good areas for walking as well as an opportunity to enjoy the traditional Broads landscapes and the wildlife that live there. Dogs are allowed on public rights of

Time and Tide.

way under close control, but many nature reserves do not allow access for dogs. The nature reserves are generally open daily.

Alderfen Broad (page 43) *Near Neatishead, 3 km (2 miles) east of Hoveton, Norfolk NR12 8XT (telephone 01603 625540; www.norfolkwildlifetrust.org.uk).* Water lilies, wildfowl, dragonflies and damselflies. Footpaths around the reserve and a boardwalk to the water's edge. Muddy paths all year round.

Ant Broads and Marshes (page 39) *Close to the villages of Irstead, Barton Turf and Neatishead, on the A1151, Norfolk NR29 5DD (01603 625540; www.wildlifetrust. org.uk).* Wildfowl, fen and woodland. One of the best examples of unpolluted valley fen in western Europe. Circular boardwalk near Irstead.

Barton Broad (page 39) *Near Neatishead, 2 km (1 mile) north of Hoveton, Norfolk NR12 8XP (01603 625540; www.norfolkwildlifetrust.org.uk).* The second largest broad and site of the Millennium project, Clearwater 2000, which has restored the water quality and landscape of the broad. Boat trips on the *Ra*, a solar powered boat. Wheelchair access and disabled toilet.

Breydon Water and Berney Marshes
(pages 55 and 54) *Near Halvergate and Great Yarmouth (no access by road), part of the Halvergate Marshes area, access by train from Norwich or Great Yarmouth (Berney Arms Station) or by footpath from Halvergate or Great Yarmouth, Norfolk NR31 9HU (01493 700645; www.rspb.org.uk).* Breydon Water is the confluence of the Rivers Yare and Waveney, before they join the River Bure. Visitors can see geese, ducks and waders. Berney Marshes is a huge expanse of grazing marsh, home to thousands of ducks, geese and swans in winter, and lapwings and redshanks in the spring.

Broads Wildlife Centre (page 43) *On Ranworth Broad, signposted from B1140 at South Walsham, Norfolk NR13 6HS (01603 27049; www.norfolkwildlifetrust.org.uk).* This floating wildlife centre is situated at the end of an informative boardwalk. Ferry boat available in afternoons, Apr–Oct only. Fabulous views from the centre, where there are interactive displays and children's activities. Refreshments available. Wheelchair access and disabled toilet. *The nature reserve is open all year; the wildlife centre is open Apr–Oct, daily 10.00–17.00.*

Bure Marshes (page 43) Fen, broads and fen woodland. The Bure Marshes reserve lies on either side of the River Bure, between Wroxham and Ranworth. The site includes four broads: Hoveton Great Broad (*see* page 43), Decoy Broad, Ranworth Broad and Cockshoot Broad (*see* below).

Carlton Marshes (page 66) *Burnt Hill Lane, Lowestoft, Suffolk NR33 8HU (01502 564250; www.suffolkwildlife.co.uk).* Suffolk Broads Wildlife Centre and walks across the grazing marshes. A regular haunt of wintering waders and birds of prey. Water vole can be seen among the dykes. Regular events, including children's activity days during school holidays. Wheelchair access and disabled toilet. Dogs on leads only. *Telephone for centre opening times.*

Cockshoot Broad (page 43) *Adjacent to Ranworth Broad and near Woodbastwick, Norfolk NR12 8BF (01603 625540; www.norfolkwildlifetrust.org.uk).* A boarded walkway to a bird hide overlooking the broad. The site of a pioneering project to restore clear water and wildlife, and renowned for the water lily beds and damselflies. Wheelchair access.

Hickling Broad (page 40) *Part of the Upper Thurne broads and marshes, approximately 4 km (2.5 miles) south of Stalham, Norfolk NR12 0BW (01692 598276; www.norfolkwildlifetrust.org.uk).* The largest expanse of open water in the Broads. There is a boarded walkway to the broad, together with walking trails, boat trips, and

Farmland at Ludham.

a visitor centre. Excellent views of raptors from the raptor roost at Stubb Mill *Oct–Mar*. Wheelchair access and disabled toilet. *Reserve open daily 10.00–17.00; visitor centre open Apr–Sep*.

Horsey Mere (page 41) *Horsey, Great Yarmouth, Norfolk NR29 4EF (01263 740241; www.nationaltrust.org.uk)*. Open water, reed beds, grazing marshes and a wildfowl sanctuary. Horsey wind pump (*see* page 88) is located here and there are waymarked circular walks.

Hoveton Great Broad (page 43) *Part of Bure Marshes. No access by road, reached by water from moorings on the River Bure beside the entrance (0845 600 3078; www.naturalengland.org.uk)*. A trail through woodland on the edge of the broad.

How Hill (page 44) *Near Ludham, Great Yarmouth, Norfolk NR29 5PG (01692 68555; 01692 678763 for boat trips; www.broads-authority.gov.uk)*. A National Nature Reserve of fen, grazing marsh and woodland. Walking trails and boat trips onboard the *Electric Eel*. There are three wind pumps on the reserve and Toad Hole Cottage Museum (*see* page 90). *Open Apr–May and Oct, daily 10.30–17.00; Jun–Sep, daily 09.30–18.00*.

Ludham Marshes (page 44) *On the north side of the River Thurne, between Ludham and Potter Heigham, Norfolk NR29 5PU (01603 610734; www.broads-authority. gov.uk)*. Grass marshes and an important wetland site of traditionally managed grazing marsh and dyke, with water plants, dragonflies, ducks and waders.

Martham Broad (page 46) *Martham, near Winterton-on-Sea, Norfolk NR29 4EB (01603 625540; www.norfolkwildlife trust.org.uk)*. Open water, reed and sedge fen. In summer a good place to see swallowtail butterflies. Public footpaths (muddy) to the north and south.

Mid Yare Nature Reserve (page 51) *North and south of the River Yare, near*

Strumpshaw Fen, 5 km (3 miles) east of Norwich, Norfolk NR13 4HW (01603 661662; www.rspb.org.uk). Fen, woodland, grazing marsh, open water, dykes and reed beds, all supporting wintering and breeding wildfowl, wigeon, marsh harriers, and butterflies, including the swallowtail. Nature trail and hides at Strumpshaw.

Oulton Marshes (page 66) *Reached by path from Oulton Church or by water from Oulton Dyke, Suffolk NR32 3PS (01473 890089; www.suffolkwildlifetrust.org.uk)*. Grazing meadows, fen habitat and dykes and pools, with a variety of wetland plants and breeding birds.

Strumpshaw Fen (page 51) *On the River Yare near Brundall, Norwich, Norfolk NR13 4HS (01603 715191; www.rspb.org.uk)*. Reed beds, grazing marshes, meadows and woodland. Opportunities to see marsh harriers, bitterns and kingfishers, dragonflies and butterflies, including the swallowtail. Walking trails (muddy and wet in winter) and hides. Wheelchair access and disabled toilet.

Turf Fen wind pump at How Hill.

Surlingham Church Marsh (page 51) *Near Surlingham Church, Norwich, Norfolk NR14 7DF (01603 715191; www.rspb.org.uk).* A former grazing marsh with pools, dykes and summer marsh and meadow flowers. Marsh harriers, kingfishers, water rails, and reed and sedge warblers may be seen. Circular walk and bird hides.

Upton Fen (page 44) *North of Acle off the A47, near Upton Broad, Norfolk NR29 3BT (01603 625540; www.wildlifetrust.org.uk).* Walks through tangled fen and woodland. Marsh harrier and water vole can be seen all year round and the fen is also a good place to see dragonflies. Waymarked trail (muddy all year) and boardwalk.

Ted Ellis Nature Reserve (page 57) *Wheatfen Broad, The Covey, off The Green, Surlingham, Norwich, Norfolk NR14 7AL (01508 538036; www.wheatfen.org).* Ted Ellis was a writer and broacaster who lived at Wheatfen Broad for 40 years. Wheatfen Broad is one of the last tidal marshes of the once extensive swamp area of the Yare Valley, and is an extremely sensitive site. Events throughout the year (*see* website). Some paths suitable for wheelchairs.

Winterton Dunes (page 46) *Near Winterton-on-Sea, Norfolk NR29 4AS (0845 600 3078; www.naturalengland.org.uk).* Dunes, heath, grassland, birch woodland and beach. This area is unusual because it has great ecological similarities to the dune systems of the Baltic rather than the geographically closer dunes along the Norfolk Coast. Natterjack toads breed in pools, which are also used by dragonflies. Many different species of breeding and over-wintering birds can be seen. Refreshments, toilets and parking available at Winterton-on-Sea car park.

★ OTHER PLACES TO VISIT

BeWILDerwood (page 43) *Horning Road, Hoveton, Norfolk NR12 8JW (01603 783900; www.bewilderwood.co.uk).* A wild and imaginative adventure park for both children and grown ups, with treehouses, zip wires, jungle bridges, boat trips and marsh walks. It is the setting for the children's book *A Boggle* at BeWILDerwood, by local author Tom Blofeld. Broadland Cycle Hire (*see* page 71) offers bike hire from the car park. Meals and snacks available. Picnic areas and lots of seating. Disabled play equipment and facilities but upper woodland area is naturally sloping and may be difficult to access. Guide dogs only. *Open Apr–Oct, daily 10.00–16.30/17.30; also open school holidays during February and March; closed some Tues and Weds, please check before visiting. Charge.*

Barton House Railway (page 42) *Hartwell Road, The Avenue, Wroxham, Norfolk NR12 8TL (01603 722858; www.bartonhouse railway.org.uk).* The golden age of the steam railway is re-created at this site beside the River Bure, with two ride-on railways, authentic tickets and museum of railway artefacts. The signal box was originally built in 1901 at Honing Station, and visitors can watch the signalman at work. Home baking and light meals. *Open Apr–Oct, third Sun in every month and Easter Mon, 14.30–17.30. Charge.*

Bure Valley Railway (Wroxham page 52) *Aylsham Station, Norwich Road, Aylsham, Norfolk NR11 6BW (01263 733858; www.bvrw.co.uk).* Narrow gauge railway

BeWILDerwood.

running both steam and diesel locomotives between Aylsham and Wroxham, with connections to Broads boat trips at Wroxham (maximum of two dogs allowed per boat). The railway runs alongside the Bure Valley cycle and footpath, and cycles can be carried aboard scheduled services. Restaurant and souvenir shop. Wheelchair access to Aylsham and Wroxham stations, including shops, toilets, café, platforms and Aylsham workshops; specially designed coaches accommodate wheelchairs; disabled toilet. Well behaved dogs welcome. *Open Easter-Oct, telephone or visit website for timetable. Charge.*

Fairhaven Woodland & Water Garden (page 44) *School Road, South Walsham, Norfolk NR13 6DZ (01603 270449/270683; www.fairhavengarden.co.uk).* 53 hectares (131 acres) of ancient woodland, water gardens and a private broad, described as a garden for all seasons. Tea-room *(see* Eating Out, page 29), children's trail, plant sales and boat trips. Wheelchair access to 90 per cent of gardens (including boat trips), mobility scooters available to borrow, disabled toilet. *Open all year, daily (except Christmas Day), 10.00–17.00 or dusk, whichever is earlier; also May–Aug, Wed–Thu until 21.00. Charge.*

Fritton Lake (page 60) *Beccles Road, Fritton, Great Yarmouth, Norfolk NR31 9HA (01493 488288; www.somerleyton.co.uk).* Boat trips and rowing boats for hire, children's activities including indoor barn games and a Viking fort, gardens (including a maze) and nature trails, swimming, golf, fishing and pony rides. The lake forms part of Somerleyton Estate which encompasses Somerleyton Hall *(see* page 87). Pub and tearoom. All areas of the hall and gardens are wheelchair accessible. Disabled toilet. *Open Apr–Oct, Thu and Sun; mid-Jul–Sep, also Tue and Wed; and B Hols: gardens and tea room 10.00–17.00, hall 11.30–15.30. Charge.*

Hoveton Hall Gardens (page 43) *1.5 km (1 mile) north of Wroxham, Norwich, Norfolk NR12 8RJ (01603 782558;*

www.hovetonhallgardens.co.uk). A delightful 6 hectares (15 acres) of woodland and walled gardens, water garden and lake. Tearoom and plant sales. Majority of the gardens are suitable for wheelchair access. Guide dogs only. *Open Easter Sun-early Sep, Wed, Fri, Sun and B Hol Mons (also Thu, May-Jun), 10.30-17.00. Telephone or check website before visiting. Charge.*

Great Yarmouth Row Houses (page 55) *111 South Quay, Great Yarmouth, Norfolk NR30 2RG (01493 857900; www.english-heritage.org.uk).* The narrow lanes of the Yarmouth Rows, a feature of the older part of the town, were originally a network of alleyways connecting the dwellings crammed inside Yarmouth's town walls. Many of the Row houses were damaged by World War II bombing or demolished after the war, but these surviving dwellings have been restored as fascinating museums. *Open Apr-Sep, daily 12.00-17.00. Charge.*

Pettitts Animal Adventure Park (page 59) *Church Road, Reedham, Norfolk NR13 3UA (01493 700094; www.pettittsadventurepark.co.uk).* Exotic and domestic animals and birds, animals to feed, children's rides, magic and clown shows. Café and snack bar with picnic benches designed with wheelchairs and buggies in mind. Wheelchair access and disabled toilet. *Open Apr-Oct, daily 10.00-17.00. Charge.*

Pleasurewood Hills (page 67) *Leisure Way, Corton, Lowestoft, Suffolk NR32 5DZ (01502 586000; www.pleasurewoodhills. com).* An award-winning theme park. Thrill rides and white-water adventures, including the tallest rollercoaster in the east of England. Also shows, less demanding family rides and a miniature railway. Tearooms. Disabled access. *Guide dogs only. Open Apr-Aug and school holidays in Sep and Oct, daily from 10.00. Charge.*

Sea Life Centre (page 55) *Marine Parade, Great Yarmouth, Norfolk NR30 3AH (01493 330631; www.sealife.co.uk).* Many native species and a tropical ocean display.

Visitors can eyeball all kinds of underwater creatures, from shrimps to sharks. Wheelchair access and disabled toilet. *Open all year, daily from 10.00. Charge.*

Thrigby Hall Wildlife Gardens (page 54) *Filby, near Great Yarmouth, Norfolk NR29 3DR (01493 369477; www.thrigbyhall. co.uk).* Beautifully landscaped gardens and a specialised collection of animals, birds and reptiles. Attractions include a Willow Pattern Garden, Lime Tree Lookout and the Tiger Tree Walkway constructed in the tree tops above the tigers' enclosure. Wheelchair access and disabled toilet. *Open all year, daily from 10.00. Parking and children's play areas free, charge for admission to Wildlife Gardens.*

Whitlingham Country Park (page 50) *Whitlingham Lane, near Trowse, Norwich NR14 8TR (01603 632307; www.whitlinghamoec.co.uk/www.south-norfolk.gov.uk).* Beautiful countryside encompassing the River Yare. Walking and cycling trails, bird watching, visitor centre, café and toilets. The Whitlingham Outdoor Education Centre is located here and offers a wide range of land and water based activities including sailing, windsurfing, climbing and archery. Wheelchair access and disabled toilet. All terrain wheelchairs available for loan, telephone *01603 617332* to book. *Open all year, daily. Admission free, charge for activities.*

Wroxham Barns (page 42) *Tunstead Road, Hoveton, Norfolk NR12 8QU (01603 783911; www.wroxhambarns.co.uk).* Craft studios, plant centre, farmers' market, children's farm and funfair, all set in and around restored barns and agricultural buildings. Restaurant. Wheelchair access and disabled toilet. Guide dogs only. *Open all year, daily 10.00–17.00. Admission free. Charge for children's farm and funfair (children under three go free).*

Yesterday's World (page 55) *34 Marine Parade, Great Yarmouth, Norfolk NR30 2EN (01493 331148; www.yesterdaysworld.co.uk).* A re-creation of a Victorian street and shops. Visitors can immerse themselves in Victorian life and children can enjoy a ride on a Victorian carousel, dating from 1889. Tearoom and gift shop. Disabled access and toilet. *Open Mar–Oct, daily 10.00–17.00. Charge (free for children under four).*

Places to Visit

ACKNOWLEDGEMENTS

Photographs marked BA are reproduced by kind permission of the Broads Authority.
Photographs marked NNSS are © Crown Copyright 2009, GB Non-Native Species Secretariat.
Photographs marked FGT are reproduced by kind permission of the Fairhaven Gardens Trust.
Photographs marked S courtesy of Shutterstock.
Cover image; Norfolk Broads, Hunsett Mill, Pictures Colour Library, Brian Lawrence Images Ltd.

2, BA; 4, BA; 5–7 corners, S, Laurence Gough; 5, BA; 6, BA; 7, S, Laurence Gough; 8, BA; 9–13 corners, S, Joy Fera; 9, BA; 10, S, jeff gynane; 12, BA; 13, S, wheatley; 14, S, Keith Levit; 15–17 corners, S, Paul Cowan; 16, BA; 17, S, Darren Pierse Kelly; 19 corner, S, Stephen Finn; 20 S, Christopher Elwell; 21–23 corners, S, maga; 21, BA; 22, foopath sign, S, Mark William Richardson; 22, Broads walk sign, BA; 23, S, Laurence Gough; 25–27 corners, BA; 27, FGT; 29 corner, S, Kati Molin; 31–37 corners, S, Laurence Gough; 37, S, Paul Cowan; 39–69 corners, S, David Hughes; 41, S, David Hughes; 45, BA; 47, S, Richard Bowden; 48, BA; 52, S, Shaun Robinson; 56, BA; 58, S, Richard Bowden; 61, S, Mike J Roberts; 62, S, Horia Bogdan; 63, S, Terry Alexander; 64, S, Le Do; 67, S, Anglian Art; 68, BA; 69, S, David Hughes; 71–75 corners, BA; 77–85 corners, BA; 76, BA; 77, Bearded tit, S, Cosmin Manci; 77, Bewick's swan, S, Robbie Taylor; 77, Bittern, S, Borislav Borisov; 77, Long-tailed tit, Paul Huggins; 78, Marsh harrier, S, iliuta goean; 78, Reed warbler, S, Iurii Konoval; 78, Treecreeper, S, Sue Robinson; 78, Wigeon, S, Terry Alexander; 78, Willow tit, S, Kristof Degreef; 79, Bream, S, Dewitt; 79, Perch, S, Krasowit; 79, Pike, S, Silvia Iordache; 79, Rudd, S, Gala_Kan; 80, Comma butterfly, S, willmetts; 80, Common darter Dragonfly, BA; 80, Banded demoiselle, Paul Huggins; 80, Glow worm, timo_w2S; 80, Norfolk hawker, S, Ainars Aunins; 81, Swallowtail, S, Marek Mierzejewski, 81, Brown hare, S, Pavel Mikoska; 81, Daubentons bat, Mike Lane; 81, Harvest mouse, S, Eric Isselée; 81, Otter, S, JKlingebiel; 82, Red deer, S, Ewan Chesser; 82, Water vole, laurencea; 82, Buckler fern, S, Drahomír Kalina; 82, Cross-leaved heath, S, Ainars Aunins; 82, Early marsh orchid, S, Ainars Aunins; 83, Grey Willow, S, Cosmin Manci; 83, Guelder rose, S, Malgorzata Kistryn; 83, Ragged robin, S, Steven Paul Pepper; 83, Meadow thistle, S, RTimages; 83, Yellow water lily, S, Gregory Johnston, 84, American mink, NNSS; 84–85, Hickling Broad, BA; 85, Himalayan Balsam, NNSS; 85, Japanese knotweed, S, Steve McWilliam; 85, Zebra mussels, S, David P. Lewis; 87–89 corners, Wroxham Barns; 86, S, Shaun Robinson; 91 corner, FGT; 88, Beccles & District Museum; 89, East Anglia Transport Museum; 90, Norfolk Museums and Archaeology Service, David Kirkham; 91, BA; 92, BA; 93–95 corners, S, David Hughes; 93, BeWILDerwood.

INDEX